SMALL BITES BIG FLAVOR

SMALL BITES

BIG FLAVOR

CHEF ERIC LeVINE

Simple, Savory and Sophisticated Recipes for Entertaining

FOREWORD
BY DAVID BURKE

PHOTOGRAPHS
BY TONY CALARCO

LYONS PRESS
Guilford, Connecticut
An imprint of Globe Pequot Press

Consumer Advisory: Consuming raw or undercooked meats, poultry, seafood, shellfish, or eggs may increase your risk of foodborne illness, especially if you have certain medical conditions.

Project editors: Tracee Williams and Ellen Urban
Text design and layout: Nancy Freeborn

Library of Congress Cataloging-in-Publication Data

LeVine, Eric.
 Small bites big flavor : simple, savory and sophisticated recipes for entertaining / Chef Eric LeVine ; foreword by David Burke ; photographs by Tony Calarco.
     pages cm
 Summary: "Accolades from the James Beard Foundation, the International Chefs Association, the judges of Chopped, and more attest to the energy, imagination, and passion of Chef Eric LeVine's cuisine, here delivered in a beautiful, personality packed cookbook filled with delicious recipes, perfect for entertaining on any scale"—Provided by publisher.
 Includes index.
 ISBN 978-0-7627-9132-3 (hardback)
1. Entertaining. 2. Appetizers. 3. Cooking. 4. Flavor. I. Title.
 TX731.L479 2013
 642'.4—dc23
                          2013032435

Printed in the United States of America
10 9 8 7 6 5 4 3 2 1

CONTENTS

BIG BITES 115

Entree-Style: Heartier Dishes for Entertaining with a Twist

SWEET BITES 159

Simple and Elegant Desserts for Every Occasion

TASTY COCKTAILS 197

Balancing Flavor in Delectable Drinks

FOREWORD

I can't think of a more exciting time than right now to be a chef in America. The media and the country as a whole are having a love affair with food, and chefs have taken on "rock star" status. While fame among the masses and respect among your peers don't come easily in this industry, those with talent, drive, and the guts to go for it do find their success. In my book, there's no better example of the creative, tenacious chef than Eric LeVine.

I met Eric before this food revolution, in the early 1990s when he came to work for me at the River Café in Brooklyn. He was a fellow graduate of the Culinary Institute of America, and I welcomed him into the kitchen and hoped he had potential. The River Café is a tough testing ground. It is a New York City icon known for really raising the bar when it comes to the modern interpretation of classic cuisine—developing flavor profiles, sourcing local and seasonal ingredients, demanding perfection.

From the beginning, I knew Eric would succeed. He was an eager, curious student and was detail oriented. He was willing to take both advice and criticism and use them to get better. At the same time, he wasn't afraid to make a suggestion or try something new. Like me, he was a kid in a candy store when it came to food—experimental, creative, and passionate. But he also had a great respect for ingredients and for the fundamentals of good cooking.

In time, Eric left the River Café. He knew that it was time to build his culinary repertoire abroad, and he spent time working with top chefs in France, Italy, and Japan. He kept in

Note:

All recipes requiring salt use kosher salt; all recipes using pepper use white pepper unless otherwise indicated.

All presentations shown within these pages are concepts—feel free to use your own ideas! If you have questions, contact me via my website, ChefEricLeVine.com.

Experience Level
① = Easy
② = Medium
③ = Advanced

touch, and when he returned I could tell that he'd matured; he'd further built that crucial foundation that a good chef must learn to honor before he can successfully interpret—or put his own "spin" on—ingredients and recipes. And most important, he'd learned to trust his instincts. I wasn't surprised when the awards and accolades started pouring in for him.

Eric has developed his niche over the years, gaining respect as a restaurateur, caterer, consultant, and teacher. He's mastered the concept of "small plates"—recipes that pack flavor and creativity into one bite. He's also become a "chef's chef"—someone who enjoys the process as much as the result, who rises to the challenge but is always willing to learn more. With *Small Bites Big Flavor,* he further solidifies his spot among the nation's best. These are recipes that are worth the effort, not just because they taste good, but because they challenge the home cook to think more like a professional chef—to find great ingredients, interpret them creatively, and present them beautifully. I am proud to call Eric a colleague and, when you get right down to it, a guy whose food I really enjoy.

David Burke

FIRE IT UP!

The flavors of the kitchen, the experience of creating, the joy of sharing. Many of our favorite memories start with friends and family gathering over a beautiful meal, sharing their love and laughter.

Never before has an opportunity to share with you meant so much to me as a chef and member of our human family. As a five-time cancer survivor, I know just how precious life is and am grateful for every day I have to share my kitchen wisdom with you. Whatever chance you have, open your home and your heart to friends and family, creating the gift of a new memory. Take that bite out of life now!

Open your life to all types of gifts. For me, the greatest gift I can give someone is a meal. When I take special care with a recipe, pouring all my love into every step, and finishing the plate with specific detail, I am telling that recipient, Thank you for being here—you matter, and I care. It's my gift of love, friendship, and fellowship.

Most of us remember our mom's party food: pigs in a blanket, port-wine cheese and crackers, maybe a slow cooker filled with Swedish meatballs. *Small Bites Big Flavor* pays homage to these iconic dishes but are twisted into modern tastes that are simple to prepare yet will wow your guests. Each of the recipes has options to make the dishes uniquely yours.

It's these childhood memories that often inspire the meals we make. My grandma and mom cooking for me were some of the most calming times for a kid living in a chaotic world. My grandma's honey cake (page 194) and my mom's kalamata hummus (page 86) are culinary touchstones that never fail to make me smile.

Thank you for allowing me to share this book with you. Every recipe is written with love and the hope that you will take time out of your crazy-busy life to create fun, inspired memories for your friends and families.

Live in the moment, and fire it up!

Eric

SMALL BITES
Hors d'Oeuvres

When I was a young cook working for a catering company in Brooklyn, New York, I prepared thousands of appetizers on any given day. Every item came with detailed instructions from the executive chef on how to prepare and execute it, but, as a test to see if I was paying attention, he never gave me the full list of ingredients. Thankfully, I was. In fact, I would often improve on his recipes by cutting out unnecessary steps and tweaking them with ingredients he left off the list.

This challenge showed me the importance of being prepared, trusting my instincts, and keeping a recipe as simple as possible. That's my hope for you, too, with my small-bites recipes. They all start with three main ingredients that I've used in three different recipes. I call it the 3 x 3 approach, and it gives you a starting point from which you can add your own touches and ideas.

Small bites set the tone for the party, creating festive and fun tastes for all of you to enjoy. You should have as much fun making them as your guests will have eating them! Think of small bites as little kisses from your kitchen. Put all of your love into them, and fire it up!

MUSHROOM GINGER CHICKEN CREPE CUP

The flavors of chicken, ginger, and mushroom have always been a great combination in various cultures and many cuisines. This light and flavorful twist on a classic presentation will delight your guests.

CREPES

⅓ cup all-purpose flour

½ teaspoon salt

3 eggs

1 cup milk

Preheat oven to 350°F.

Grease mini muffin tins with nonstick spray.

In a large bowl, whisk the flour, salt, eggs, and milk until smooth. (You can also use a blender.)

Heat a lightly greased 8-inch nonstick skillet; add a tablespoon of batter to make about a 3-inch round. Lift and tilt pan to evenly coat bottom. Cook until the top appears dry, 1–2 minutes. Place crepe in a greased muffin cup. Repeat with the remaining batter. Bake in oven for 6–8 minutes until slightly browned. Remove crepes from muffin tin and hold until ready to fill.

MUSHROOM RAGOUT

1 pound mixed mushrooms, such as shiitake, cremini, and white button

2–4 tablespoons unsalted butter

1 medium shallot or ½ small onion, chopped

½ teaspoon salt

Freshly ground black pepper to taste

3 sprigs fresh thyme, leaves stripped, plus more sprigs for presentation

½ cup Madeira or white wine

⅓ cup heavy cream

Clean the mushrooms by brushing with a kitchen towel or a brush to remove any loose dirt. Remove the shiitake stems and discard. Trim the dry ends off the cremini and white mushroom stems. Quarter all the mushrooms and set aside in a bowl.

Heat 2 tablespoons butter in a large skillet over medium-high heat. Add the mushrooms, spread them out evenly in the pan, and increase the heat to high. Let the mushrooms cook undisturbed until they brown, then shake the pan to turn them over. Add additional butter along the sides of the pan if the pan seems very dry as the mushrooms cook. Continue to cook until nicely browned, about 5 minutes. Add the shallot and cook until softened, about 2 minutes. Season the mushrooms with the salt and pepper and add the thyme leaves. Pull the pan off the heat and add the Madeira or white wine. Return pan to the heat and, with a wooden spoon, scrape up any of the brown bits that cling to the bottom of the pan. Add the heavy cream and bring to a boil. Remove from the heat.

CHICKEN

1 pound chicken tenders

1½ tablespoons peeled and grated ginger

2 tablespoons olive oil

Heat oven to 350°F. Toss tenders with grated ginger and olive oil and bake for 10–12 minutes. Remove from oven and allow to cool. Shred and reserve for assembly.

ASSEMBLY:

Scoop ½ teaspoon mushroom ragout into each crepe cup, then top with 1 teaspoon of shredded chicken and serve on a tray garnished with thyme. These bites can be served room temperature, or warm them by heating the filled crepe cups in a 350°F oven for 2–3 minutes.

CHEF'S NOTES:

The ragout mixture can be made a few days ahead without affecting the quality; this will only intensify the layers of flavor.

VARIATIONS:

The chicken can be replaced with pork and/or shrimp.

BEST SEASON:

The earthy tones of the wild mushroom ragout are perfect for a crisp fall or cold winter's night. Serve with a nice glass of Pinot Noir.

SPRING ROLL–STYLE GINGER-MARINATED PULLED CHICKEN WITH MUSHROOM

This small bite is created in the style of a spring roll but uses the French crepe technique. It lends itself to a cross-culture of flavors, as the crepe is an unexpected foil for the zing of ginger and Szechuan pepper oil.

EXPERIENCE LEVEL: ③
YIELD: 20 BITES

CREPES

1½ cups all-purpose flour

1 teaspoon salt

6 eggs

2 cups milk

In a large bowl, whisk the flour, salt, eggs, and milk until smooth. (You can also use a blender.)

Heat a lightly greased 8-inch nonstick skillet. Add 6 tablespoons batter; lift and tilt pan to evenly coat the bottom. Cook for 1–2 minutes until the top appears dry. Remove from the pan and let cool on a sheet pan. Repeat with the remaining batter until you have 10 crepes.

GINGER-MARINATED PULLED CHICKEN

2 chicken breast halves with skin and bone
    (1½ pounds total)

1½ teaspoons fresh lime juice

1 teaspoon Asian chili-bean paste with garlic
    (preferably Lan Chi)

1 teaspoon red chili oil, or to taste

1 teaspoon Szechuan pepper oil, or to taste

1 teaspoon finely grated peeled fresh ginger

½ teaspoon finely grated peeled garlic

½ teaspoon minced fresh mild long red chile pepper,
    such as Holland

½ teaspoon salt

1 cup fresh cilantro leaves

1½ cups chicken stock

1 tablespoon cornstarch for thickening (optional)

Lightly rinse chicken and pat dry. Combine all ingredients except cornstarch in a bowl, and toss chicken to lightly coat. Allow to marinate for 2 hours in an airtight container in refrigerator.

Place chicken in a pressure cooker and cook for 30–40 minutes, or cook in a pot with a tight-fitting lid in the oven at 350°F for 1 hour. Remove and let cool on a wire rack; reserve the cooking liquid. Remove skin and shred the chicken off the bone.

Strain the cooking liquid and heat on medium high for 15–20 minutes, until it reduces to about 1 cup; thicken with cornstarch slurry if the liquid has not naturally thickened. Let cool, and fold in just enough to coat chicken mixture, about ¾ cup, reserving the remainder.

VEGETABLE JULIENNE

6 snow peas, julienned

1 (2-ounce) package enoki or shiitake mushrooms

½ carrot, peeled and julienned

1 scallion, sliced diagonally to make 4-inch pieces

1 teaspoon reduced cooking liquid from Ginger-
    Marinated Pulled Chicken

Toss together. Drizzle just enough reduction to coat the vegetables. Reserve in refrigerator for assembly.

ASSEMBLY:

Place a crepe on top of the work surface. Lay about 2 tablespoons of chicken mixed with sauce in the center of the crepe. Top the chicken with a scoop (about 1 tablespoon) of the vegetable mixture. Fold the crepe over, then fold the crepe flaps in and roll to create a spring roll. Cut in half before serving and "tie" each piece with a narrow strip of green scallion top.

CHEF'S NOTES:

This item cannot be rolled ahead of time or the moisture will seep into the crepes, making them soggy.

The crepes can be made one day ahead and held in an airtight container at room temperature.

VARIATIONS:

Changing the chicken for pork, veal, or shrimp makes a fun alternative.

You can also change the crepe flavor with scallion and sesame seeds, or add cilantro or basil—use your imagination!

BEST SEASON:

This is best in warmer weather (spring or summer), depending on the freshness of the key ingredients.

STIR-FRIED MUSHROOMS WITH SHREDDED GINGER CHICKEN IN WONTON PURSES

This great "purse" bite can enhance a cocktail party or be fun just on its own. It may take a little practice, but once you get the hang of it, forming the purses will go quickly.

EXPERIENCE LEVEL: ②
YIELD: 20 BITES

CHICKEN FILLING

2 chicken breast halves with skin and bone
    (1½ pounds total)
1½ teaspoons fresh lime juice
1 teaspoon Asian chili-bean paste with garlic
    (preferably Lan Chi)
1 teaspoon red chili oil, or to taste
1 teaspoon Szechuan pepper oil, or to taste
1 teaspoon peeled and finely grated fresh ginger
½ teaspoon peeled and finely grated garlic
½ teaspoon minced fresh mild long red chile,
    such as Holland
½ teaspoon salt
1 cup fresh cilantro leaves
1½ cups chicken stock
1–1½ tablespoons cornstarch, for thickening (optional)

Lightly rinse chicken and pat dry. Combine all ingredients except cornstarch in a bowl and toss chicken to lightly coat. Allow to marinate at room temperature for 2 hours in airtight container.

Place chicken in a pressure cooker and cook for 30–40 minutes, or cook in a pot with a tight-fitting lid in a 350°F oven for about 1 hour. Remove and let cool on a wire rack. Remove skin and, using a fork, shred the chicken from the bone. Strain the sauce, return to the heat, and reduce to about 1 cup, thickening with cornstarch slurry if the liquid has not naturally thickened. Fold into chicken just enough sauce to moisten, about ¾ cup. Cool and reserve remaining sauce.

DIPPING SAUCE

3 cloves garlic, minced
2 tablespoons peeled and minced fresh ginger
¾ cup olive oil
⅓ cup rice vinegar
½ cup soy sauce
3 tablespoons honey
¼ cup reserved chicken reduction sauce

Combine in a blender and turn on to medium speed. Slowly incorporate water to emulsify and stabilize the dressing.

STIR-FRY MUSHROOMS

2 teaspoons sesame oil
1 tablespoon chopped garlic
½ tablespoon peeled and grated ginger
½ cup sliced shiitake mushrooms
½ cup enoki mushrooms, separated and ends
    removed
2 tablespoons soy sauce

Heat sesame oil in wok or saucepan over medium heat. Add garlic and ginger, stirring constantly to lightly brown. Add mushrooms and sauté until tender, adding soy at finish (do not reduce soy too much or it will intensify the salt flavor). Remove from head and reserve for wonton assembly.

CHICKEN WONTONS

20 (4 x 4-inch) wonton skins
2 eggs
2 tablespoons water
2 quarts canola oil for frying

Place 4 wonton skins at a time on a work surface. Combine eggs and water to make a wash, and brush the outside ¼ inch of each wonton square. Fill the center of the wonton skin with a scant teaspoonful of chicken filling topped with ½ teaspoon of mushroom stir-fry, allowing enough room to pull all four corners into the center to form the purse—they will stick together. Repeat with the remaining wonton skins and reserve for frying.

ASSEMBLY:

In a 4-quart saucepan heat 2 quarts oil to 350°F. Drop each purse into the fryer and cook until golden brown, 3–4 minutes. Remove and place on paper towel to drain. Serve warm with small bowls of dipping sauce.

CHEF'S NOTES:

When working with wonton skins, keep them covered with a damp paper towel.

Wonton purses can be made and frozen up to a month ahead of cooking. If you don't want to fry them, coat them with cooking spray and bake in a 350°F oven for 15–20 minutes if frozen, less if room temperature.

VARIATIONS:

Substitute egg roll skins or thin sheets of fresh pasta for the wonton skins.

BEST SEASON:

This dish is delicious anytime due to year-round availability of the ingredients.

CRAB SALAD ROLLED IN DAIKON RADISH WITH SESAME SAUCE

This Pacific Rim—inspired hors d'oeuvre offers a balance of texture and flavor. The raw-radish wrap complements the delicate crabmeat, and the nuttiness of sesame plays perfectly off the slight heat of the wasabi to make the perfect bite.

EXPERIENCE LEVEL: ②
YIELD: 10 BITES

CRAB, DAIKON RADISH, RED RADISH 3 X 3

SESAME SAUCE

2 tablespoons soy sauce
1 tablespoon Dijon mustard
¼ teaspoon sesame oil
¼ teaspoon peeled and grated fresh ginger
2½ teaspoons water

Combine all ingredients in a blender and mix until smooth. Place in a small sauce bowl or ramekin and reserve at room temperature.

CRAB SALAD ROLL

1 medium daikon radish
1 teaspoon wasabi paste
1 tablespoon mayonnaise
⅛ teaspoon salt
4 small fresh basil leaves, cut into thin strips
½ cup cooked crabmeat
½ medium avocado, cut into 10 pieces
2 tablespoons julienned carrot
2 red radishes, julienned
1 bunch snow pea sprouts or bean sprouts

Shave the daikon radish into ten 4-inch lengths on the thinnest mandoline setting to create long, thin daikon radish sheets. Drop them into ice water, and reserve.

Combine wasabi paste, mayonnaise, salt, and cut basil; slowly and lightly fold the crabmeat into the mayonnaise mixture.

ASSEMBLY:

Place a daikon radish sheet on a work surface. Place a teaspoon of the crab mixture on one end. Top the crab with a piece of avocado and an even amount of julienned carrot and red radish. Top with 3 or 4 snow pea sprouts. Drizzle with a few drops of sesame sauce. Roll tightly toward the other end of the daikon radish. When all rolls are assembled, reserve in an airtight container in the refrigerator.

CHEF'S NOTES:

This item can be prepared a few hours before serving if kept covered and refrigerated.

VARIATIONS:

You can substitute zucchini or cucumber for the daikon radish.

BEST SEASON:

This lighter spring and summer dish can be a great hors d'oeuvre or salad course when entertaining.

PICKLED DAIKON RADISH DISC WITH CRAB DIP AND RED ONION CONFIT

This creamy crab dip is a robustly flavored delight. The pickled daikon and the onion confit lend a sweet and sour element to this rich bite. Be sure to start the onions early in the day, as they take six hours to pickle.

EXPERIENCE LEVEL: ②
YIELD: 20 BITES

RED ONION CONFIT

1 pint red pearl onions, peeled
1 cup Alessi Pinot Grigio Wine Vinegar
1 cup sugar
1 cup orange juice
2 teaspoons pickling spices

Combine ingredients in a large saucepan. Heat over a low flame to a slow simmer. Turn off and allow the onions to steep for 6 hours. Once onions have steeped, drain and discard liquid.

PICKLED DAIKON RADISH

1 daikon radish
1 cup Alessi Pinot Grigio Wine Vinegar
1 cup sugar
1 cup orange juice
2 teaspoons pickling spices

Using a mandoline, slice radish into ¼-inch-thick pieces. Then, using a 1½-inch-diameter cookie cutter, punch out rounds. Combine all ingredients in a saucepan and lightly poach for about 2–3 minutes, until daikon is slightly tender. Remove from liquid, chill on a plate in refrigerator, and reserve.

CRAB DIP

1 (8-ounce) package cream cheese, softened
1 cup mayonnaise
½ teaspoon lemon juice
2 teaspoons Old Bay Seasoning, more if desired
½ teaspoon ground mustard
1 pound lump crabmeat, picked over for shells
¼ cup shredded cheddar cheese

Preheat the oven to 350°F. Mix cream cheese, mayonnaise, lemon juice, Old Bay Seasoning, and ground mustard in a medium bowl until well blended. Add crabmeat; toss gently. Spread in a shallow 1½-quart baking dish. Sprinkle with cheddar cheese and additional Old Bay Seasoning, if desired. Bake for 30 minutes or until hot and bubbly. Cool and reserve.

ASSEMBLY:

Slice several of the pickled onions crosswise into rings and set aside. Place each daikon radish disc on the work surface. Spoon ½ teaspoon crab dip onto the disc and top with 3 onion-confit rings.

CHEF'S NOTES:

All items can be made and refrigerated up to three days in advance.

VARIATIONS:

Add some soy sauce to the daikon radish poaching liquid for a little more flavor.

Instead of crab dip you can use artichoke dip or chicken bacon dip. Garnish with chopped green celery leaf.

BEST SEASON:

Spring and summer are great times for this item. The piquancy of the pickling would be complemented by a nice glass of Pinot Noir or an IPA.

CRAB PURSE WITH RADISH DIPPING SAUCE

The "tie" for this luxurious crab-filled crepe purse is the dark green part of the spring onion. A swim in simmering water makes the scallions pliable, and shocking them in a bowl of icy water stops the cooking and retains their vibrant color for a dramatic effect.

EXPERIENCE LEVEL: ②
YIELD: 20 BITES

CREPES

⅔ cup all-purpose flour

½ teaspoon salt

3 eggs

1 cup milk

6 scallions

In a large bowl, whisk the flour, salt, eggs, and milk until smooth. (You can also use a blender.)

Lightly grease an 8-inch nonstick skillet with cooking spray and place over medium heat; add 3 tablespoons batter to form an 8-inch crepe. Lift and tilt the pan to evenly coat the bottom. Cook until the top appears dry, 1–2 minutes. Remove from pan and cool on sheet pan. Repeat with the remaining batter.

Cut the green tops off the scallions and lightly poach them in water for about 30–45 seconds, until they turn a vibrant green. Shock the drained greens in ice water. Remove from water, dry, and cut each lengthwise into thin strips. Set aside.

CRAB MIX

1 (8-ounce) package cream cheese, softened

½ cup mayonnaise

½ teaspoon ground mustard

½ teaspoon lemon juice

1 pound lump crabmeat, picked over for shells

In a mixing bowl, combine cream cheese, mayonnaise, mustard, and lemon juice. With a rubber spatula fold together until smooth. Lightly fold crabmeat into mixture, being careful not to mash the crabmeat. Reserve, covered and refrigerated.

RADISH DIPPING SAUCE

½ cup mayonnaise

2 teaspoons ketchup

5 red radishes, chopped fine

¼ teaspoon paprika

¼ teaspoon salt

⅛ teaspoon dried oregano

Dash of ground black pepper

Cayenne pepper to taste

Combine all ingredients in a blender and puree until smooth. Reserve, covered and refrigerated.

ASSEMBLY:

Place a crepe on the work surface and spoon 1 generous tablespoon crab mix into the center. Pull the edges of the crepe shell into the middle. Wrap the crepe about ½ inch from the top edge with a strip of blanched scallion green and tie it loosely. Repeat for the remaining crepes.

Fill a small ramekin with the radish dipping sauce and serve with the purses.

CHEF'S NOTES:

All of the components can be put together a day or two ahead of time. Before filling the crepes, warm them in the oven for 2 minutes at 250°F. This will allow for a more flexible crepe and keep it from cracking when gathered up.

VARIATIONS:

Spinach dip or hummus can be used instead of crab mix.

BEST SEASON:

This item is best for spring and summer.

PORK ROULADE STUFFED WITH MARINATED ARTICHOKE AND RICOTTA

In this recipe a pork tenderloin is butterflied and rolled with artichokes and ricotta. It's wrapped in plastic and foil before being roasted, which keeps the meat moist. Because the pork is pounded thin, searing it and roasting it uncovered would dry out the meat.

1 (12–16-ounce) pork tenderloin

Salt and pepper to taste

1 (12-ounce) jar marinated artichoke hearts, drained

1 cup packed basil leaves

1 cup ricotta cheese

½ cup grated Parmesan

2 large eggs

Butterfly the pork tenderloin and season with salt and pepper. Lay it on a 12 x 12-inch piece of plastic wrap. Place another piece of plastic wrap over the tenderloin and pound it to a ¼-inch thickness. Discard the top piece of plastic.

Place artichoke hearts, basil, ricotta cheese, Parmesan, and eggs in a food processor and pulse until slightly smooth but still chunky. Spread the mixture evenly on the tenderloin, except for 1 inch on the right-hand side. Roll the pork from left to right; the right-hand inch of meat seals the tenderloin. Wrap in plastic, being sure to twist the ends tightly. Roll the pork roulade in a 12 x 12-inch piece of aluminum foil, again twisting the ends.

Preheat the oven to 300°F. Roast the roulade on a baking sheet for 20–25 minutes or until the internal temperature is 150°F. Remove foil and plastic and allow to cool. Cut the cooled tenderloin into ½-inch slices and serve.

CHEF'S NOTES:

The roulade can be made two days in advance. To ensure the best results, be sure that you twist both ends of the foil before you place the roulade in the oven.

VARIATIONS:

Chicken can be used as a substitute for the pork.

BEST SEASON:

This is a perfect fall item to serve with a good IPA.

ARTICHOKE STUFFED WITH PORK AND RICOTTA

These marinated artichoke hearts are filled with fresh ricotta cheese and a sauté of rosemary, bacon, and ground pork. They are then breaded in panko and fried. Who doesn't want this?

EXPERIENCE LEVEL: ②
YIELD: 12 BITES

6 marinated artichoke hearts, halved

½ pound bacon

3 teaspoons chopped garlic

2 teaspoons olive oil

½ pound ground pork

Sprig of fresh rosemary, leaves removed and chopped

Salt and pepper to taste

1 cup ricotta cheese

1 cup all-purpose flour

6 eggs

2 cups panko bread crumbs

2 quarts canola oil for frying

Basil leaves, chopped, for garnish

Drain artichokes from marinade and dry them. Cook bacon until golden brown; cool, dice, and reserve.

Sauté garlic in olive oil until light brown. Add ground pork and rosemary, season with salt and pepper, and cook through; allow to cool. In a bowl combine the ricotta, pork mix, and bacon. Mix thoroughly.

Fill the inside of each half artichoke with a teaspoon of the mix. Put in freezer for 10 minutes to firm before you begin the breading process.

ASSEMBLY:

Set up your breading bowls in a line from left to right: flour in the first, eggs beaten with 3 tablespoons water in the second, and panko bread crumbs in the third. Use your left hand for dry ingredients and your right hand for wet ingredients, as follows. Use your left hand to roll the stuffed artichoke in the flour. Remove it, transfer it to your right hand, and place it in the egg, turning to be sure all sides are well covered. Still with your right hand, remove it and drop it into the panko. With your left hand, shake the panko bowl to cover the artichoke on all sides, then remove it from the bread crumbs and place it on a tray. Repeat with each artichoke half.

In a 2-gallon stockpot, heat frying oil to 350°F and fry the artichokes until they float, about 3–5 minutes. Remove and place on paper napkins to absorb oil. Shingle on a serving plate and serve on their own, or drizzle with garlic aioli (see below) and finish with chopped basil.

GARLIC AIOLI

¾ cup mayonnaise

3 cloves garlic, minced

2½ tablespoons lemon juice

¾ teaspoon salt

Pepper to taste

Mix all ingredients in a bowl. Cover and refrigerate at least 30 minutes before serving.

CHEF'S NOTES:

These can be breaded a week ahead, wrapped well, and frozen. They may be fried direct from frozen. The leftover filling may also be frozen for later use.

VARIATIONS:

Instead of using ground pork, use ground chicken or chopped shrimp.

BEST SEASON:

This is a great fall or winter item. It can be paired with a Sauvignon Blanc or Pinot Grigio.

ARTICHOKE SALAD WITH PULLED PORK AND GARLIC-RICOTTA AIOLI

This tasty forkful is sure to be a crowd pleaser. The delicate flavors of the artichoke salad, which is infused with the flavors of the rich pork and zesty garlic aioli, make this bite-size treasure a party in your mouth.

EXPERIENCE LEVEL: ②
YIELD: 20 BITES

ARTICHOKE SALAD

1 (12-ounce) jar marinated artichoke hearts, drained and chopped
½ red onion, peeled and finely diced
8 ounces mushrooms, sliced, sautéed in 1 tablespoon butter, and cooled
3 tablespoons olive oil
Salt and pepper to taste

Combine all ingredients, mix well, and refrigerate until ready to assemble.

PULLED PORK

2 pounds boneless pork roast
1 tablespoon Cajun seasoning
1 tablespoon unsalted butter
1 medium onion, chopped
4 cloves garlic, crushed
4 cups water
1 tablespoon liquid smoke flavoring

Cut the pork roast into large chunks and season generously with Cajun seasoning. Melt butter in a large skillet over medium-high heat. Add the pork and brown on all sides. Remove from the skillet and transfer to a slow cooker.

Add the onion and garlic to the skillet, and cook for a few minutes until tender. Stir in the water, scraping up the browned pork bits from the bottom of the pan. Pour the whole mixture into the slow cooker with the pork. Stir in liquid smoke flavoring.

Cover, and cook on high for 6 hours, or until meat falls apart when pierced with a fork. Remove pieces of pork from the slow cooker and shred. Cool and reserve.

GARLIC-RICOTTA AIOLI

½ cup mayonnaise
¼ cup ricotta cheese
3 cloves garlic, minced
2½ tablespoons lemon juice
¾ teaspoon salt
Pepper to taste

Mix all ingredients in a bowl. Cover and refrigerate at least 30 minutes before serving.

ASSEMBLY:

On a fork, layer small dollops of garlic-ricotta aioli, artichoke salad, and pulled pork and serve.

ARTICHOKE, PORK, RICOTTA 3 X 3

CHEF'S NOTES:

Everything can be prepared up to two days in advance; assemble up to an hour before serving.

VARIATIONS:

Use grilled chicken, or add 1 tablespoon chopped chipotle pepper for a little heat.

BEST SEASON:

Fall, with a Pinot Noir.

TURBOT KNÖDEL, ENGLISH PEA PUREE, AND THYME-LEMON SHEETS

The delicate yet firm turbot is wonderful in this Bavarian-style bread dumpling. The savory acidity of the lemon and thyme complements the sweetness of the peas and the fresh fish.

EXPERIENCE LEVEL: ②
YIELD: 12 BITES

TURBOT

4 slices day-old white bread
⅓ cup milk, plus more as needed
6 ounces turbot fillet
Salt and pepper to taste
2 tablespoons olive oil
¼ cup minced onion
2 tablespoons minced parsley
¼ teaspoon dried marjoram
2 teaspoon butter
1 egg
¼ teaspoon freshly grated nutmeg
¼ cup English peas

Preheat oven to 350°F.

Cut or tear the bread into small bits. Pour ⅓ cup milk over the bread and let it sit 5 minutes. Test and see if it needs more milk; the bread should be softened but not dripping wet. Add enough milk to achieve this consistency; the actual amount depends on how dry the bread is.

Season turbot with salt and pepper, drizzle with oil, and roast in oven for 8–12 minutes until flaky. Let cool, and flake lightly with a fork.

Sauté the onion, parsley, and marjoram in butter until softened.

Combine the egg and nutmeg with the bread, then add the sautéed onion and the peas, and mix. Fold the fish in. Let the mixture rest for 10 minutes, then mix again briefly; taste, and add more herbs if necessary. The dough should be firm, with pieces of the bread crust still visible.

With wet hands, form 12 knödels (round dumplings, about 1 inch in diameter) and cook 15–20 minutes in simmering water; do not let the water boil. They are done when they feel firm and float to the top. You can make knödels in any size, but adjust the cooking time accordingly. Keep warm.

ENGLISH PEA PUREE

½ cup English peas
1 cup vegetable stock
Salt and pepper to taste

Place peas in a blender and slowly add stock to create a thick puree. Season with salt and pepper to taste.

THYME-LEMON SHEETS

1 lavash sheet
1 lemon
Sprig of thyme, leaves removed

Bake lavash in 350°F oven for 3–4 minutes, until crisp.

Cut lemon in half and squeeze juice onto the lavash. Brush evenly to coat the entire top. Chop thyme leaves and sprinkle evenly on top of the lavash. Cut lavash into 1-inch squares.

ASSEMBLY:

Spread a small amount of pea puree on each lavash crisp, top with a warm knödel, skewer (I use one from Pick On Us), and serve.

CHEF'S NOTES:

The knödels can be made a day in advance and reheated in the oven.

VARIATIONS:

You can substitute other proteins such as cooked chicken, shrimp, salmon, or pork for the fish in the knödel mixture.

Using different-flavored stocks in the pea puree, or adding mayonnaise and garlic to create a pea aioli, changes the experience also.

BEST SEASON:

Best served during the fall and winter seasons.

TOMATILLO TURBOT TACO

Who doesn't love an adorable bite-size taco? This south-of-the-border favorite takes a tour of the South of France by pairing zesty tomatillo salsa with sweet-pea aioli and the essence of lemon and thyme.

EXPERIENCE LEVEL: ②
YIELD: 10–12 BITES

TURBOT

½ pound turbot

1 cup prepared salsa

3 tomatillos, peeled and chopped

1 bunch cilantro, leaves removed and chopped

6 tablespoons lime juice

½ cup chopped red onion

2 jalapeño peppers, seeds and ribs removed, and chopped

Mix together all ingredients except turbot. Cut turbot into paper-thin pieces. Toss into salsa mixture and marinate, covered in the refrigerator, 6–8 hours or overnight.

PEA AIOLI

½ cup English peas

3 tablespoons mayonnaise

2 teaspoons chopped garlic

1 teaspoon fresh-squeezed lemon juice

Salt and pepper to taste

Place all ingredients in a blender, and puree until smooth.

THYME AND LEMON TACO

2 (12-inch) flour tortillas

Juice of 1 lemon

2 fresh thyme sprigs, leaves removed and chopped

Cut tortillas into 2-inch rounds. Brush with lemon juice and sprinkle with thyme.

Preheat the oven to 325°F.

Fold a 10-inch-long piece of aluminum foil into a bending wave to create five V-shapes to hold and shape 10–12 tortillas into tacos. Or use a straight-line baking rack with half-inch space in between, and slightly bend the taco shell to fit between the bars of the cooling rack. Place the 2-inch rounds in the "waves," set on a sheet pan, and bake for 20 minutes or until crisp. Remove from oven and let cool.

ASSEMBLY:

Place mini tacos on a tray. Fill with turbot-salsa mixture and pea aioli (or serve on the side).

CHEF'S NOTES:

The taco shells can be made days ahead and frozen. Remove from freezer 30 minutes before needed.

VARIATIONS:

Change the turbot to snapper for a variation. Use tomato instead of tomatillos, but be sure to decrease the lime juice to 4 tablespoons because the tomatoes are more acidic.

BEST SEASON:

Spring and summer are best seasons for this dish. Enjoy with a nice Pinot Grigio.

TURBOT CEVICHE, PEA SALAD, AND LEMON CRISP

Ceviche is one of my favorite fish preparations. This South American–inspired technique allows the freshness of the fish to shine.

EXPERIENCE LEVEL: ②
YIELD: 12–15 BITES

TURBOT CEVICHE

½ pound turbot
4 tablespoons lime juice
2 tablespoons diced red onion
4 tablespoons small-diced seeded tomatoes

Dice turbot into small pieces, but do not mash. Toss with lime juice, red onion, and tomato. Refrigerate 5–6 hours before serving.

PEA SALAD

¼ cup fresh peas
1 medium shallot, shaved
2 teaspoons olive oil
Salt and pepper to taste

Toss all ingredients together and set aside.

LEMON CRISPS

3 (6-inch) corn shells
1 lemon
1 sprig thyme, leaves removed

Preheat the oven to 300°F.

Cut corn shells into 2-inch rounds. Zest lemon into a bowl, and squeeze its juice in also. Chop thyme leaves and add to lemon juice/zest, creating a light paste. Brush the paste onto corn rounds and bake in oven for 10 minutes.

ASSEMBLY:

Place the corn circles on a tray. Place a small amount of turbot ceviche on each crisp and top with pea salad.

CHEF'S NOTES:

Crisps can be made two days in advance but must be kept in an airtight container with a sprig of thyme for additional flavor.

VARIATIONS:

Use scallops, tuna, or *hamachi* as a variation for the fish. Instead of using peas, use bean sprouts for a light crunch and flavor.

BEST SEASON:

This item is best served on the warm days of late spring and summer.

GINGER-BRAISED DUCK AND PICKLED-PLUM ROLLS

Duck begs for flavors like ginger and sweet plums. The pickled plum relish balances the savory sweetness of the tender duck wraps.

EXPERIENCE LEVEL: ②
YIELD: 12 BITES

BRAISED DUCK

1 whole Muscovy duck, approximately 3 pounds

Salt and pepper to taste

2 cups hoisin sauce

3 cups chicken stock

½ cup flour

3 teaspoons peeled and grated ginger

½ cup tomato paste

3 celery stalks, chopped

2 large carrots, peeled and chopped

1 Spanish onion, peeled and chopped

½ cup oil

6 (6-inch) flour tortillas, for assembly

Season the duck with salt and pepper, then sear in a large sauté pan on all sides until golden brown.

In a saucepan, combine the hoisin, stock, flour, ginger, and tomato paste, and bring to boil.

Preheat the oven to 250°F.

Place celery, carrot, and onion in the bottom of a roasting pan that just holds the duck. Place the seared duck on top. Pour the hoisin-stock mixture over the duck to cover with just the top peeking out of the liquid. Cover the pan with parchment paper and aluminum foil, and bake for 2–2½ hours, or until fork tender. Remove the duck from the liquid and allow to cool for 10 minutes. Remove any fat from outside of duck, then shred the duck with a fork. Keep warm.

PICKLED PLUMS

3 plums, split and pitted, skin on

1 cup Alessi White Balsamic Pear Infused Vinegar (or any quality Champagne vinegar)

1 cup orange juice

1 cup sugar

½ cup pickling spices

Slice plums ⅓ inch thick. Combine all ingredients in a saucepan. Heat mixture to 160°F and turn off. Allow to cool, then remove plums from pickling liquid and reserve for assembly.

ASSEMBLY:

Lightly grill tortillas on both sides. Spread 2 tablespoons pulled duck down the center of each tortilla. Place 4 slices of pickled plum on top of the duck, roll the tortilla, cut in half, and serve.

CHEF'S NOTES:

This can be served with a barbecue aioli for a little more punch.

VARIATIONS:

Substitute chicken prepared in the same fashion as the duck, pulling it from the bones after braising.

BEST SEASON:

This item is great year-round, especially when served with a light craft beer.

DUCK SALAD WITH PICKLED PLUMS AND PLUM-GINGER JAM

Plums macerate with sugar and ginger until all of the flavors meld and they are made into a jam. It pairs well with this spiced duck salad, served in a spoon or in a bamboo cone (I use one from Pick On Us).

EXPERIENCE LEVEL: ②
YIELD: 15–18 BITES

DUCK

2 (8–10-ounce) Muscovy duck breasts
2 tablespoons olive oil
2 tablespoons chopped garlic
1 tablespoon peeled and grated fresh ginger
½ cup bean sprouts, reserving a few for garnish
½ cup shredded carrots
Fresh sprouts for garnish

Preheat the oven to 350°F. Score the skin of each duck breast with a knife.

Combine oil, garlic, and ginger in a bowl and mix well. Rub both sides of the duck breasts with mixture. Roast the duck breasts, skin side down, on a sheet pan for 10–15 minutes or until cooked to the desired temperature (115–120°F is medium rare). Remove from rendered fat and allow to cool. Remove skin and any remaining fat, slice the duck breast thin, julienne the slices, and toss with bean sprouts and carrots. Refrigerate until assembly.

PICKLED PLUMS

3 plums, split and pitted, skin on
1 cup Alessi White Balsamic Pear Infused Vinegar
    (or any quality Champagne vinegar)
1 cup orange juice
1 cup sugar
½ cup pickling spices

Slice plums ⅓ inch thick. Combine all ingredients in a saucepan. Heat mixture to 160°F and turn off. Allow to cool, then remove plums from pickling liquid and reserve for assembly.

PLUM-GINGER JAM

1 pound plums, washed, pitted, and roughly chopped
¾ cup granulated sugar
3 (¼-inch-thick) slices of peeled fresh ginger
¼ lemon, seeds removed

In a medium-size, nonreactive saucepan, toss the plums with the sugar and the ginger slices and let stand, stirring occasionally, until the sugar is mostly dissolved, about 1 hour.

Squeeze the lemon over the plums, then add the chunk of lemon to the saucepan and bring to a boil, stirring until the sugar is fully dissolved. Cook over moderate heat, stirring constantly, until the liquid runs off the side of a spoon in thick, heavy drops, 20–25 minutes. Cool and reserve, covered, at room temperature.

ASSEMBLY:

Place portion of the duck salad (½ to 1 tablespoon, depending on serving vessel), a spoon or in a small cone and top with two slices of plum; next add a small dollop of jam on top of the plums. Garnish with fresh sprouts.

CHEF'S NOTES:

To add another flavor profile, finish with chopped mint.

VARIATIONS:

Use chicken in place of duck, and pear as a substitute for the plum.

BEST SEASON:

This dish is great for fall.

DUCK WRAPPED IN PICKLED PLUMS WITH PLUM-GINGER DIPPING SAUCE

This is a landlubber's sushi roll and may be served skewered (I use one from Pick On Us).

EXPERIENCE LEVEL: ②
YIELD: 12–16 BITES

DUCK

2 (8–10-ounce) Muscovy duck breasts

2 tablespoons olive oil

2 tablespoons chopped garlic

1 tablespoon peeled and grated fresh ginger

Preheat the oven to 350°F.

Score the skin of the duck breasts with a knife. Combine oil, garlic, and ginger in a bowl and mix well. Rub both sides of the duck breasts with the mixture. On a sheet pan, roast duck breasts, skin side down, 10–15 minutes or until cooked to desired temperature (115–120°F is medium rare). Remove from rendered fat and allow to cool.

PICKLED PLUMS

6 large plums

1½ cup plum sake

1½ tablespoons peeled and grated ginger

1½ cup rice vinegar

Split the plums in half along the seam and remove the pits. Using a mandoline, slice each plum into thin ⅛-inch circles. Combine all ingredients in a saucepan. Heat mixture to 120°F and remove from heat; allow to cool.

PLUM-GINGER DIPPING SAUCE

1 cup plum sauce

2 teaspoons peeled and grated fresh ginger

1 scallion, sliced

1½ tablespoons ponzu

Combine all ingredients and mix thoroughly.

ASSEMBLY:

Lay a 9 x 9-inch piece of plastic wrap on the work surface, "shingling" the sliced plums on top to create a 6 x 6-inch-square bed. Slice the duck breasts lengthwise to make 4 duck loins from each breast. Lay the duck loins at one edge of the plums and roll. Repeat for second roll. Skewer the finished rolls and cut into 1-inch pieces. Serve with the dipping sauce.

CHEF'S NOTES:

All of the components can be made two to three days ahead. You can make the rolls one day ahead and wrap them in plastic wrap, but do not cut until needed.

VARIATIONS:

You can use chicken or other game birds for this bite. Shrimp can also be used for a twist.

BEST SEASON:

Spring and summer would be best, as plums are at their peak.

GRILLED AND CHILLED ASPARAGUS-SKEWERED SHRIMP WITH ALMOND VINAIGRETTE

Chilled shrimp and asparagus are a classic combination, and here the asparagus spear is the skewer! Make sure not to overcook the shrimp; the asparagus should be crisp yet tender.

EXPERIENCE LEVEL: ③
YIELD: 8 BITES

SHRIMP SKEWERS

½ cup olive oil

2 teaspoons chopped garlic

2 teaspoons chopped fresh rosemary

½ teaspoon red pepper flakes

Pinch of salt

8 large shrimp, peeled, deveined, and tail removed

8 pencil-thin asparagus

Combine the oil, garlic, rosemary, red pepper flakes, and salt in a bowl.

Place the shrimp on the work surface and push a skewer through the shrimp horizontally from head through tail. Once you have made a hole, remove the skewer and carefully run a piece of asparagus through, bottom end first, to create an asparagus "skewer."

Marinate the shrimp in the oil-herb mixture, covered and refrigerated for at least 1 hour.

Prepare a grill on medium heat. When hot, cook the shrimp-asparagus skewers for 3–4 minutes on each side, depending on grill. Chill the shrimp-asparagus skewers until ready to serve.

ALMOND VINAIGRETTE

½ cup slivered blanched almonds

¼ cup olive oil

2 tablespoons freshly squeezed lime juice

2 tablespoons water

½ teaspoon salt

¼ teaspoon freshly ground black pepper

Preheat the oven to 350°F. Spread the almonds on a baking sheet and bake until slightly golden, about 5 minutes. Set aside to cool.

When the almonds are cool, transfer to a blender along with the remaining ingredients. Puree until smooth.

ASSEMBLY:

Serve shrimp skewers cold, with the almond vinaigrette in a small dipping bowl or ramekin.

CHEF'S NOTES:
Be sure to use large shrimp (about 12–15 per pound) for this item.

VARIATIONS:
Instead of shrimp, you can use chicken or even beef tenderloin.

BEST SEASON:
This is a refreshing warm-weather dish, so spring and summer are optimal times.

SHAVED SHRIMP AND ASPARAGUS SALAD WITH ALMOND AIOLI

This is a refreshing addition to any hors d'oeuvres display. The thin slivers of raw asparagus mirror the shaved poached shrimp, allowing for consistent distribution when tossed with the toasted almond dressing.

EXPERIENCE LEVEL: ②
YIELD: 8–10 BITES

SHRIMP

½ pound shrimp, peeled, deveined, and tails
    removed
2 cups water
1 cup white wine
¼ cup fresh-squeezed lemon juice

Combine all ingredients in a saucepan. Bring the temperature to 130°F. Once shrimp begin to change color, remove pan from heat and allow shrimp to steep for 20 minutes until cooked all the way through. Remove shrimp from the liquid and cool in refrigerator.

Once shrimp are cool, use a sharp chef's knife to rough-chop the shrimp. Set aside.

ASPARAGUS SALAD

6 pencil-thin asparagus spears
3 teaspoons olive oil
2 teaspoons Alessi White Balsamic Pear Infused
    Vinegar (or any quality Champagne vinegar)
1 teaspoon chopped garlic
Salt and pepper to taste
1 scallion, thinly sliced on the bias
1 vine-ripened tomato, seeds removed, cut into
    ¼-inch dice

Cut off the ends of the asparagus spears, cut each one in half at the middle of the stalk, and shave the asparagus using a peeler into a bowl.

Combine oil, vinegar, garlic, salt, and pepper to make the dressing. Toss asparagus, scallion, and tomato with the dressing.

ALMOND AIOLI

½ cup mayonnaise
2 teaspoons lemon juice
1 teaspoon chopped garlic
2 teaspoons finely chopped toasted almonds

Combine all ingredients in a bowl and whisk together. Refrigerate.

ASSEMBLY:

Combine the cooled shrimp and asparagus salad in a bowl, mixing well to incorporate the ingredients. Taste and adjust seasoning if needed. Portion the salad into a small cup or bamboo cone (I use one from Pick On Us), and top with almond aioli.

CHEF'S NOTES:

This is one of those dishes that can have a fun presentation and fun flavors; it goes well with a Chardonnay or Pinot Noir.

VARIATIONS:

Use chicken or pork for this light salad.

BEST SEASON:

This is best during asparagus season in late spring and summer.

POACHED SHRIMP AND ASPARAGUS SUSHI ROLL
WITH PONZU-ALMOND DIPPING SAUCE

Japan meets California in this sushi roll. The shrimp is cooked, making this an ideal hors d'oeuvre for those who are squeamish about eating raw fish. Be aware that you need to start this recipe four weeks in advance.

EXPERIENCE LEVEL: ③
YIELD: 8 BITES

PONZU-ALMOND DIPPING SAUCE

¼ cup sake (preferably Dassai 50)

¼ cup mirin

½ cup bottled yuzu juice

½ cup *katsuobushi* (bonito flakes)

6 tablespoons soy sauce

1 (5 x 5-inch) piece kombu

1 cup chopped almonds

10 cherry leaves, optional

Place sake and mirin in a small saucepan; bring to a boil. Let boil for 30 seconds. Transfer to an airtight container along with yuzu juice, *katsuobushi,* soy sauce, kombu, and chopped almonds. Cover and refrigerate for 3 weeks.

Strain the mixture through a fine-mesh sieve and discard the solids. Return the mixture to an airtight container and add cherry leaves. Cover and refrigerate for 1 week before using.

SHRIMP AND ASPARAGUS ROLL

1 nori sheet

1 cup cooked sushi rice

4 steamed shrimp, halved lengthwise head to tail

2 asparagus spears, blanched and cut in half

1 tablespoon toasted sesame seeds

Pickled ginger, wasabi, and soy sauce for serving

Cover the sushi mat with plastic wrap to prevent sticking. Lay the nori on top of the covered mat. Wet your hands with cold water and press the sushi rice on top of the nori, leaving a 1-inch space empty on the edge of the nori closest to you. Place the shrimp and asparagus spears in a thin horizontal line across the middle of the rice. Wet hands again with the water and, with the help of the sushi mat, roll the rice toward you in a jelly-roll fashion. Be sure to roll tightly, but without too much pressure, to ensure an even sushi roll.

Unwrap the sushi mat. Place the toasted sesame seeds on a clean plate. Roll the sushi roll in the toasted sesame seeds to cover. Using a clean and sharp knife, cut the roll into 8 pieces. Serve with pickled ginger, wasabi, and light soy sauce.

CHEF'S NOTES:

Ponzu sauce can be purchased; add chopped almonds or almond extract for quick flavor.

VARIATIONS:

Instead of using shrimp, you can also use seared tuna loin dusted with some Chinese chili powder.

BEST SEASON:

This light dish is best served in warm weather and can be enjoyed with a chilled sake.

CHICKEN AND BACON ROULADE WITH MUSTARD DIP

This baked chicken and bacon hors d'oeuvre is on the healthier side without sacrificing flavor. The zippy mustard dip and smoky bacon add complexity. Pound the chicken thin between two pieces of plastic wrap for a consistent thickness.

EXPERIENCE LEVEL: ②
YIELD: 12–14 BITES

CHICKEN ROULADE

1 pound boneless, skinless chicken breasts or jumbo chicken tenders

8 smoked bacon strips

3 teaspoons mustard powder

Preheat the oven to 325°F.

Clean the chicken breasts and butterfly them. Place them on a 12 × 12-inch piece of plastic wrap and top with another 12 × 12 piece. Pound the chicken to an approximate ⅛-inch thickness. Remove the top plastic; the chicken should be about 8 × 8 inches.

Lay the bacon on the chicken, leaving ½ inch of the closest and farthest sides empty. Roll the chicken in the plastic to form a roulade. Wrap in aluminum foil, set into the preheated oven and cook for 20–25 minutes. Remove from oven when the chicken reaches an internal temperature of 145°F, and allow to rest for 10 minutes.

Remove from foil and plastic. With a sharp slicing knife (not serrated) cut into ½-inch slices and skewer (I use one from Pick On Us). Serve warm or at room temperature with dip.

MUSTARD DIP

½ cup prepared yellow mustard

3 teaspoons cooked and chopped bacon

1 teaspoon reserved bacon fat from cooked bacon

1 teaspoon chopped flat-leaf Italian parsley

Combine all ingredients in a bowl and mix well to incorporate. Refrigerate until ready to serve.

CHEF'S NOTES:

This dish can be made a day or two ahead of time and refrigerated whole until ready to serve. The dip can be made five days in advance. Makes a great middle-of-the-night snack!

Do not use a serrated knife to slice the roulade, as this will shred the chicken.

VARIATIONS:

You can change the protein and use shrimp or pork. Change the sauce and add a small amount of red chili flakes to bring some heat into the dish.

BEST SEASON:

This is great year-round with a full-flavored beer.

MUSTARD-AND-BACON-CRUSTED CHICKEN BITES WITH BACON AIOLI

I love a twisted version of fried chicken. Smoky bacon enhances this bite in two ways: It adds crunch to the mustard-spiced crust and a unique flavor to the cooling aioli.

EXPERIENCE LEVEL: ②
YIELD: 12–16 BITES

BACON AIOLI

½ cup mayonnaise

2 teaspoons fresh-squeezed lemon juice

1 teaspoon chopped garlic

4 bacon strips, cooked and roughly chopped

Combine all ingredients into a bowl and mix thoroughly. Refrigerate, covered, until ready to use.

CHICKEN BITES

4 jumbo chicken tenderloins (about 10–12 ounces total)

½ cup mustard powder

1 teaspoon chopped flat-leaf Italian parsley

½ cup cooked and chopped bacon

2 cups panko bread crumbs

6 eggs

1 cup canola oil

Roll chicken tenderloins in mustard powder. Combine chopped parsley, cooked bacon, and panko in a separate bowl. In a third bowl, beat eggs with 3 tablespoons water. Dredge the chicken in the egg wash, covering the chicken completely. Remove it from the egg wash, allow any excess liquid to drip off, and roll the chicken in panko mix until completely covered. Remove and place in refrigerator until ready to cook.

When ready to cook, heat 1 cup oil in a saucepan over medium heat and cook both sides of chicken until chicken is cooked through, about 2–3 minutes each side (internal temperature of 160°F). Cut chicken into ½-inch pieces and serve with bacon aioli.

CHEF'S NOTES:

The chicken can be breaded two weeks ahead of time and frozen in an airtight container. When you plan to use it, remove it from the freezer 1 hour prior to cooking, then follow the normal procedure.

VARIATIONS:

Use shrimp, pork, or even a zucchini stick as a variation for this fun, tasty morsel.

BEST SEASON:

Fall get-togethers and small parties are naturals for this item.

GRILLED BACON-WRAPPED CHICKEN WITH MUSTARD AIOLI

Here the bacon acts as a skin, adding moisture to the chicken as it cooks. It's crispy on the outside, juicy on the inside, and only made better with the zesty mustard dipping sauce.

EXPERIENCE LEVEL: ②
YIELD: 16 SKEWERS

MUSTARD AIOLI

½ cup prepared mustard
½ cup mayo
2 teaspoons lemon juice
1 teaspoon chopped garlic

Combine all ingredients thoroughly in a mixing bowl. Refrigerate until ready to use.

CHICKEN

8 chicken tenderloins
4 smoked bacon slices, cut in half
Salt and pepper to taste

Prepare a grill to medium heat.

Lay a piece of bacon on a work surface. Place a tenderloin on one end of the bacon. Roll chicken in a spiral, stretching the bacon so it covers the chicken. When all the rolls are prepared, grill them until the bacon is crisp but not burnt, 8–10 minutes on medium heat, not above the flame (internal temperature should be about 160°F).

ASSEMBLY:

Slice each chicken tender into four equal-size pieces, and skewer two pieces together (I use skewers from Pick On Us). Serve with aioli on the side for dipping.

CHEF'S NOTES:
The chicken can be wrapped in bacon a day in advance. Be careful when grilling; if the flame is too high, it may burn the bacon before it or the chicken cooks.

VARIATIONS:
This also can be made with pork, scallops, shrimp, or veal.

BEST SEASON:
This a great spring, summer, and fall dish.

SPICY COLD-SMOKED SALMON, CUCUMBER, AND GINGER-RICE ROULADE

Classic ingredients with a twist! These rolls explode with flavor—smoky salmon and zingy ginger create an unexpected cohesion of flavor, while the cucumber adds a fresh crunch.

EXPERIENCE LEVEL: ③
YIELD: 12–18 BITES

SPICY SALMON

1½ teaspoons mayonnaise

⅛ teaspoon Sriracha sauce

1½ teaspoons thick hot chili sauce, or to taste

¼ pound cold-smoked salmon, diced

3 sheets nori, for assembly

Stir together the mayonnaise, Sriracha, and hot chili sauce in a bowl. Add the diced salmon to the bowl, turning it over to coat it well. Refrigerate, covered, until ready to use.

CUCUMBER SAUCE

1 cup plain yogurt

Juice of 1 cucumber

2 tablespoons olive oil

Juice of ½ lemon

Salt and pepper to taste

1 tablespoon chopped fresh dill

3 cloves garlic, peeled

1 teaspoon black sesame seeds

Combine all ingredients except sesame seeds in a blender and mix until smooth. Sprinkle with sesame seeds and refrigerate until ready to use.

GINGER RICE

3 cups Japanese rice

⅓ cup peeled and grated fresh ginger

⅓ cup rice vinegar

3 tablespoons sugar

1 teaspoon salt

Put the rice in a large bowl and wash it with cold water. Repeat washing until the water becomes almost clear. Drain the rice in a colander and set aside for 30 minutes. Place rice and ginger in rice cooker and add 3¼ cups water; let rice soak at least 30 minutes more. Start the cooker. After rice is cooked, let it steam for about 15 minutes.

Prepare sushi vinegar by mixing rice vinegar, sugar, and salt in a saucepan. Put the pan over low heat, and heat until the sugar dissolves. Let cool.

Transfer the hot steamed rice to a large plate or bowl and spread it. (Use a nonmetallic bowl to prevent any reaction with rice vinegar—it's best to use a wooden bowl called *sushi-oke,* if possible). Sprinkle the vinegar mixture over the rice and fold the rice using a *shamoji* (rice spatula) quickly. Be careful not to smash the rice. To cool the rice and remove any additional moisture, use a fan as you mix sushi rice. This will give it a shiny look.

ASSEMBLY:

Center one nori sheet on a bamboo sushi mat. Wet your hands and use them to spread a thin layer of rice on the nori; press it down. Arrange one-third of the salmon in a line down the center of the rice. Lift the end of the mat, and gently roll it over the ingredients, pressing gently. Roll it forward to make a complete roll. Repeat with remaining ingredients. Cut each roll into 4–6 slices using a wet, sharp knife. Serve with cucumber sauce on the side.

CHEF'S NOTES:

When rolling, lightly wet the edge of the nori to seal the roll. To slice, use a sharp knife, not a serrated knife, which will tear the roll.

If you don't have a juicer, peel and seed the cucumber, and whirl it in a blender to puree.

VARIATIONS:

This can also be made with tuna.

BEST SEASON:

This is perfect in spring and summer with a Pinot Noir or a light beer.

MARINATED COLD-SMOKED SALMON SUSHI CUP

If you love sushi but do not have the time or talent to roll maki, you can still enjoy the flavors with this presentation. The bright coral color of the fish makes a stunning display on a buffet, and serving it in individual cups or glasses makes it easy for your guests to enjoy in a cocktail-party setting.

EXPERIENCE LEVEL: ②
YIELD: 8–10 BITES

MARINATED COLD-SMOKED SALMON

2 teaspoons sesame oil

2 teaspoons rice vinegar

1 teaspoon chopped cilantro

¼ pound cold-smoked salmon, diced

1 sheet nori, for assembly

Combine oil, vinegar, and cilantro, and mix well. Right before assembling the cup, toss diced salmon in the dressing.

SUSHI RICE

1 cup Japanese rice

1½ tablespoons rice vinegar

1 tablespoon sugar

1 teaspoon salt

Put the rice in a large bowl and wash it with cold water. Repeat washing until the water becomes almost clear. Drain the rice in a colander and set aside for 30 minutes. Place the rice in rice cooker and add 1¼ cups water; let the rice soak in the water at least 30 minutes more. Start the cooker. After the rice is cooked, let it steam for 15 minutes.

Prepare sushi vinegar by mixing rice vinegar, sugar, and salt in a saucepan. Put the pan on low heat and heat until the sugar dissolves. Let cool.

Transfer the hot steamed rice to a large plate or bowl and spread it. (Use a nonmetallic bowl to prevent any reaction with rice vinegar. It's best to use a wooden bowl called *sushi-oke*, if possible.) Sprinkle the vinegar mixture over the rice and fold the rice using a *shamoji* (rice spatula) quickly. Be careful not to smash the rice. To cool the rice and remove any additional moisture, use a fan as you mix sushi rice. This will give it a shiny look.

ASSEMBLY:

Cut nori into 4 equal pieces 1½ to 2 inches wide, then slice into fine strips. Scoop a tablespoon of rice into each cup, scoop salmon on top of rice, and sprinkle nori to garnish.

CHEF'S NOTES:

If you cannot find cold-smoked salmon, use baked salmon as a substitute.

VARIATIONS:

You can use grilled tuna, grilled shrimp, or any smoked fish, like turbot, wreckfish, or pike.

BEST SEASON:

Warm weather is the best time for this dish. Serve it with a light, fruity Chardonnay or a light sake.

SMOKED SALMON BELLY–RICE POP WITH CUCUMBER DIP

The belly is thought to be the tastiest part of the salmon because it is where the fat is stored. Folded with rich cream cheese and seasoned sushi rice, these succulent pops are served with a refreshing cucumber-lemon dipping sauce for balance.

EXPERIENCE LEVEL: ②
YIELD: 18–20 BITES

SUSHI RICE

1 cup Japanese rice
1½ tablespoons rice vinegar
1 tablespoon sugar
1 teaspoon salt

Put the rice in a large bowl and wash it with cold water. Repeat washing until the water becomes almost clear. Drain the rice in a colander and set aside for 30 minutes. Place the rice in rice cooker and add 1¼ cups water; let the rice soak in the water at least 30 minutes. Start the cooker. After the rice is cooked, let it steam for about 15 minutes.

Prepare sushi vinegar by mixing rice vinegar, sugar, and salt in a saucepan. Put the pan on low heat and heat until the sugar dissolves. Let cool.

Transfer the hot steamed rice to a large plate or bowl and spread it. (Use a nonmetallic bowl to prevent any reaction with rice vinegar. It's best to use a wooden bowl called *sushi-oke*, if possible.) Sprinkle the vinegar mixture over the rice and fold the rice using a *shamoji* (rice spatula) quickly. Be careful not to smash the rice. To cool the rice and remove any additional moisture, use a fan as you mix sushi rice. This will give it a shiny look.

CUCUMBER DIP

1 English cucumber, peeled, seeds removed, and diced
3 tablespoons fat-free plain Greek yogurt
Juice of ½ lemon
1 tablespoon chopped fresh mint

Combine all ingredients in a bowl and mix thoroughly. Refrigerate until ready to serve.

SUSHI

2 teaspoons chopped capers
1 sheet nori, chopped fine
½ pound smoked salmon belly, diced small
½ cup cream cheese, softened

ASSEMBLY:

Combine the rice, capers, nori, salmon, and cream cheese in a bowl and mix until ingredients are well incorporated. Take about 1 tablespoon of the mixture, shape into a ball, and skewer with a bamboo stick (I use one from Pick On Us). Repeat until all the mixture is used. Serve with cucumber dip.

CHEF'S NOTES:

Keep ingredients cool and work fast so this item doesn't get warm and pasty.

VARIATIONS:

You can use any fatty or high-oil-content fish for this. I would not recommend bluefish, however, as it will overpower the rice.

BEST SEASON:

This dish is best served in summer with a light Chardonnay or sake.

MINI BRAISED SHORT-RIB TACO BITES

Braised short ribs literally melt in your mouth. I love them as filling for homemade mini taco shells. The 2-inch tortillas are baked into shape using aluminum foil—so easy, and a real crowd pleaser!

EXPERIENCE LEVEL: ②
YIELD: 20–24 BITES

SHORT RIBS

3 pounds boneless beef short ribs
Salt and freshly ground black pepper to taste
¼ cup olive oil
1 large onion, diced
3 cloves garlic, peeled and coarsely chopped
1 cup tomato paste
1 cup red wine (Cabernet Sauvignon is good)
½ cup Dijon mustard
3 cups beef stock

Preheat the oven to 300°F.

Season the rib meat with salt and pepper. Heat the oil in a large, heavy-bottomed, ovenproof pan over medium heat. Add the meat in batches and brown on all sides, about 8–10 minutes. Remove browned rib meat from pan and set them aside. Add the onion and garlic to the pan and cook, stirring frequently, for 2 minutes. Add the tomato paste, wine, and mustard. Bring the mixture to a boil, scraping the brown bits from the ribs into the mixture.

Return the rib meat to the pan and add the beef stock. Cover the pan, bring to a simmer, and place in the oven for 2½ hours, until the meat shreds. Remove meat from the pan and remove any excess fat from the surface of the cooking liquid. Transfer the cooking liquid to the bowl of a food processor. Process until the mixture is a smooth sauce. Pour the sauce into a pan and keep warm over low heat.

MINI TACOS

1 (12-inch) flour tortilla
2 ounces Joan of Arc Roquefort cheese (or other quality Roquefort), crumbled
Fresh rosemary, for garnish

Preheat the oven to 325°F.

Cut tortillas into 2-inch rounds. Fold a sheet of aluminum foil into a bending wave, creating a series of V shaped troughs to hold the tortillas in a taco shape. Or use a straight-line baking rack with half-inch space in between, and slightly bend the taco shell to fit between the bars of the cooling rack. Place the 2-inch rounds in the "waves," set on a sheet pan, and bake for 20 minutes or until crisp. Remove from oven and let cool. Repeat until all taco shells are baked.

ASSEMBLY:

Shred the short rib meat and lightly toss with the warm sauce. Fill each mini taco shell with a bit of meat and top with a bit of crumbled Roquefort and rosemary.

BEEF, GARLIC, ROQUEFORT 3 X 3

CHEF'S NOTES:

Short ribs can be used in many different ways, as shown in this and the following recipes. The braised short ribs will hold in your refrigerator up to 2 weeks and in your freezer up to 3 months in a properly sealed airtight container. Makes a good omelet mix.

VARIATIONS:

Use pork or veal for a variation on this dish. The thickness of the meat will determine how long you should cook it. For every inch of thickness, estimate 45–60 minutes, depending on your oven. You can substitute beer for the red wine; a dark stout will build up the earthy flavor of this dish.

BEST SEASON:

This works well in fall and winter and is great with beer or red wine.

BRAISED SHORT RIBS WITH ROQUEFORT CHEESE MASHED POTATOES

This is a comforting dish, so robust in flavor that a small portion is perfectly satisfying. The pairing of Roquefort cheese and rich beef is a timeless classic.

EXPERIENCE LEVEL: ②
YIELD: 12–15 BITES

RED WINE–BRAISED SHORT RIBS

3 pounds boneless beef short ribs

Salt and freshly ground black pepper to taste

¼ cup olive oil

1 large onion, diced

3 cloves garlic, peeled and coarsely chopped

1 cup tomato paste

1 cup red wine (preferably Cabernet Sauvignon)

3 tablespoons Dijon mustard

2 cups beef stock

Fresh herbs and or fried onions for garnish (optional)

Preheat the oven to 325°F.

Season the ribs with salt and pepper. Heat the oil over medium heat in a large, heavy-bottomed, ovenproof pan. Add the ribs in batches and brown on all sides, about 8–10 minutes. Remove the ribs from pan and set aside. Add the onion and garlic to the pan and cook, stirring frequently, for 2 minutes. Add the tomato paste, wine, and mustard to the pan and bring the mixture to a boil, using a wooden spoon to scrape up the brown bits that cling to the bottom of the pan. Return the ribs to the pan. Add the beef stock to the pan, cover, bring to a simmer, and place in the oven for 2½ hours, until the meat falls easily from the bone. Remove the ribs from the pan, discard the bones, and cut the meat into bite-size pieces. Remove any excess fat from the surface of the cooking liquid. Transfer the cooking liquid to the bowl of a food processor and process until the mixture is a smooth sauce. Pour the sauce into a pan, add the rib meat to it, and keep warm over low heat.

ROQUEFORT CHEESE MASHED POTATOES

4 large baking potatoes, peeled and cut into 2-inch chunks

Salt to taste

12 ounces Joan of Arc Roquefort cheese (or other quality Roquefort), crumbled, divided

1 cup milk

1 cup sour cream

½ cup unsalted butter, softened

1 tablespoon dried dill weed

1 teaspoon salt

1 teaspoon freshly ground black pepper

Place the potatoes in a large pot and cover with salted water. Bring to a boil over high heat, then reduce heat to medium-low, cover, and simmer until tender, about 20 minutes. Drain and allow the potatoes to steam dry for a minute or two.

Preheat the oven to 350°F. Grease a 9 x 13-inch baking pan.

Transfer the potatoes to a food processor. Add 8 ounces Roquefort cheese, milk, sour cream, butter, dill weed, salt, and pepper. Process until smooth. Pour the mixture into the prepared baking pan. Sprinkle with the remaining 4 ounces Roquefort, then cover with aluminum foil. Bake in the preheated oven for 30 minutes. Remove foil and continue baking until the cheese is lightly browned, 15–20 minutes more.

ASSEMBLY:

Spoon some potato puree into a small wine or water glass. Place a piece of short rib meat on top of the potatoes. Place a fork in the glass and serve, garnished with herbs or fried onions, if desired.

CHEF'S NOTES:

Use this small item to offer a variety of "entree" bites to your guests.

VARIATIONS:

Pork can be used in this dish, as well as veal, chicken, or lamb. Change it up even more by using sweet potatoes instead of regular potatoes.

BEST SEASON:

This is a great fall and winter dish.

CHILI TORTILLA CRISP WITH ROQUEFORT CHEESE POLENTA AND SHORT RIBS

In this preparation, the short ribs are braised in a Dutch oven with citrus, cilantro, garlic, and jalapeño. The braising liquid is then reduced to make a flavorful glaze for the shredded beef, which is paired with creamy, earthy corn polenta.

EXPERIENCE LEVEL: ②
YIELD: 18–20 BITES

BEEF, GARLIC, ROQUEFORT 3 X 3

CHILI SHORT RIBS

3 pounds boneless beef short ribs, cut into
   4-ounce portions

3 cups *mojo*

3 cloves garlic, chopped

1 teaspoon chopped fresh cilantro

1 quart water

½ cup chili powder

½ cup jalapeños, split, seeded, and rough chopped

1 teaspoon crushed red pepper flakes

¼ cup fresh orange juice

2 tablespoons fresh lemon juice

Preheat the oven to 350°F.

In a wide stockpot or Dutch oven, combine all ingredients. Make sure the pot is deep enough so the short ribs can be fully submerged in the liquid. Cover the pot. Bake the short ribs for about 3 hours, or until the meat is tender. Remove from the oven.

Remove the short ribs from the braising liquid and cover to keep them warm. Remove fat from the surface of the cooking liquid and discard. On the stovetop over high heat, reduce the liquid until approximately 1¼ cups remain (about 20 minutes), then pour it through a fine-mesh strainer, discarding the solids. Return the short ribs and the reduced sauce to the stockpot or Dutch oven; coat the short ribs with the sauce. Increase the oven temperature to 425°F and bake uncovered for 10 minutes, until the short ribs are heated through and slightly glazed. Set aside until ready to serve.

ROQUEFORT CHEESE POLENTA

2 cups chicken stock

1 cup dry polenta

¾ cup milk

4 ounces Joan of Arc Roquefort cheese (or other
   quality Roquefort), crumbled

Pour chicken stock into a saucepan and bring to a boil. Slowly pour in the polenta while stirring vigorously. Cook for a few minutes, then stir in milk. Reduce heat to low, cover, and simmer for about 5 minutes, until thick. Stir Roquefort into the polenta until it has melted.

CHILI CRISPS

2 (12-inch) flour tortillas

2 teaspoons chili powder

2 teaspoons olive oil

½ teaspoon salt

Preheat the oven to 250°F.

Cut each tortilla into 1½-inch rounds. Combine chili powder, oil, and salt, and mix well. Brush tortilla rounds with chili mixture and place on baking sheets. Bake for 5–8 minutes, or until crisp. Remove and let cool.

ASSEMBLY:

Spoon a bit of polenta on each tortilla crisp and top with some shredded short rib.

CHEF'S NOTES:

The short ribs can be made ahead of time and reheated for serving. If you allow the short ribs to sit in the sauce, the meat will develop even better flavor.

VARIATIONS:

This dish would be great to make with pork shoulder or pork butt.

BEST SEASON:

Fall and winter are great times of year for this item. Serve it at a party with margaritas or mojitos for a little extra punch.

GREEN PEA BISCUITS WITH PROSCIUTTO AND SWEET PEA AIOLI

Starchy peas give a unique texture and slight sweetness to the biscuits in this whimsical spin on ham biscuits.

EXPERIENCE LEVEL: ②
YIELD: 24 BITES

SWEET PEA AIOLI

1 cup sweet peas
½ cup mayonnaise
2 teaspoons fresh-squeezed lemon juice
2 teaspoons chopped garlic

Combine all ingredients in a food processor and blend well. Hold until ready to assemble.

GREEN PEA BISCUITS

2¼ cups self-rising flour
¾ cup shortening
¾ cup buttermilk
½ cup pureed sweet peas

Preheat the oven to 425°F.

Place the flour in a large bowl, cut in the shortening until the pieces are small (the size of peas), add the buttermilk and pea puree, and mix ingredients together. Pour the mixture onto floured waxed paper. Pat out the dough with your hands until it is not sticky (add a little flour if necessary). Fold double on top of itself, to end up with 4 x 6-inch rectangle of dough. Cut biscuits with a biscuit cutter or a sharp knife into 12 squares. Bake on a cookie sheet for 20–25 minutes.

PROSCIUTTO

4 thin slices Prosciutto di Parma
Sprouts, chervil, or greens for garnish (optional)

Preheat the oven to 250°F.

Lay the prosciutto slices on a sheet tray lined with parchment paper. Bake for 12–15 minutes until crisp. Remove and allow to cool. Cut into biscuit-size pieces.

ASSEMBLY:

Split biscuits in half. Spread 1 teaspoon sweet pea aioli on each half and top with a prosciutto crisp. Garnish with sprouts or chervil leaf.

CHEF'S NOTES:

You can roll the biscuit dough into a sheet and bake it, cutting it afterward.

Prosciutto di Parma is recommended, but you can also use serrano ham.

VARIATIONS:

Make black pepper biscuits, horseradish aioli, and beef jerky for a variation.

BEST SEASON:

This item can be served in the spring and summer with a nice glass of Chianti or Pinot Noir.

GREEN PEA PANNA COTTA WITH PROSCIUTTO CHIPS AND BUTTERMILK AIOLI

I always love the combination of sweet peas and salty prosciutto and the sensation of a savory custard.

EXPERIENCE LEVEL: ②
YIELD: 12 BITES

GREEN PEA PANNA COTTA

Cooking spray of canola or other neutral oil

1 tablespoon agar agar flakes

1 small celery stalk, cut into chunks

2-inch sprig of fresh rosemary

1 bay leaf

½ teaspoon whole black peppercorns

¼ teaspoon whole allspice berries

2 sprigs flat-leaf Italian parsley

Table salt to taste

2 cups green peas

¼ cup heavy cream

2 tablespoons Joan of Arc Brie cheese
    (or other quality brie)

Cayenne pepper to taste

Pepper to taste

Micro greens or celery greens, for garnish

Preheat the oven to 400°F with a rack in the center. Line a rimmed baking sheet with foil. Lightly coat the cups of a 12-cup mini muffin tin with cooking spray, and set aside.

Combine 1¾ cups water, agar agar, celery, rosemary, bay leaf, peppercorns, allspice berries, parsley, and ¼ teaspoon table salt in a small saucepan. Bring to a simmer over high heat, scraping bottom of pan occasionally, then reduce heat to low. Continue to scrape the bottom of the pan occasionally, as the agar agar likes to settle, until it appears dissolved, about 6–8 minutes.

Add peas to a blender and puree. Strain the agar agar broth through a fine-mesh strainer into blender. Add heavy cream, brie, a pinch or two of cayenne, and additional water to bring the volume just above 2 cups. Blend until smooth, scraping down the sides of the blender as needed. Taste and adjust seasoning with salt, white pepper, and additional cayenne if desired, blending briefly to fully incorporate. Evenly distribute the mixture among the 12 prepared muffin cups. Tap pan several times to settle and help remove any air bubbles that may have formed. Set aside for about an hour for the agar agar to set.

At serving time, run a thin knife around edge of panna cotta, then pop each out.

PROSCIUTTO CHIPS

4 thin slices Prosciutto de Parma

Preheat the oven to 250°F.

Using a 1-inch round cutter, cut circles of the prosciutto. Place on a sheet pan with parchment paper and bake 10–15 minutes until crisp. Reserve for garnish.

BUTTERMILK AIOLI

½ cup mayonnaise made with olive oil

⅓ cup buttermilk

1 teaspoon minced garlic

2 teaspoons chopped fresh tarragon

2 teaspoons chopped fresh basil

2 teaspoons chopped fresh cilantro

Salt and freshly ground black pepper to taste

Combine all ingredients in a blender and mix until smooth and incorporated. Refrigerate.

ASSEMBLY:

Place the panna cotta on a tray, and drop a small dollop of aioli on top of each. Place a prosciutto disc on the aioli. Top with a small drop of aioli on the prosciutto crisp. Garnish with micro greens or celery greens.

CHEF'S NOTES:

The panna cotta is best served warm or at room temperature. Do not reheat it in the microwave or it will melt. Remove from muffin tin just before serving.

VARIATIONS:

This can be made with roasted garlic or broccolini panna cotta.

BEST SEASON:

This is a great dish for a fall evening with a nice Pinot Grigio.

BUTTERMILK CUPCAKE WITH PEA HUMMUS AND MARINATED PROSCIUTTO

These sweet pea cupcakes filled with sweet pea hummus will be gorgeous on your spring or summer buffet. I think prosciutto always looks best next to green, and marinating it adds moisture and a bit of heat.

EXPERIENCE LEVEL: ②
YIELD: 24 BITES

BUTTERMILK CUPCAKE

1¼ cups all-purpose flour

¾ teaspoon baking soda

Pinch of salt

5 tablespoons unsalted butter, cut into pieces

⅔ cup milk

2 eggs

1 egg yolk

¼ cup sweet pea hummus (recipe follows)

Preheat the oven to 350°F. Spray two 12-cup mini muffin tins (or one 24-cup tin) with cooking spray.

Combine flour, baking soda, and salt in a bowl; set aside.

Heat the butter and milk in a small saucepan over low heat until the butter has melted.

Beat the eggs and egg yolk in the large bowl of an electric mixer until slightly thickened and lighter in color. Gradually beat in the flour mixture on low speed just until incorporated. Slowly pour in the hot milk/butter, beating until just combined. Add sweet pea hummus and mix well. Divide batter evenly between muffin cups. Bake until a toothpick inserted into center comes out clean, about 8–12 minutes. Cool the cupcakes in the pan for 10 minutes, then transfer to a wire rack to cool completely.

SWEET PEA HUMMUS

1 cup sweet peas

¼ cup chickpeas, drained

½ cup tahini

½ teaspoon ground cumin

2 teaspoons lemon juice

1½ cups olive oil

Place sweet peas, chickpeas, tahini, and cumin in a food processor. Process while slowly adding lemon juice, then slowly add oil. Blend until smooth.

MARINATED PROSCIUTTO

4 ounces prosciutto, thinly sliced

½ teaspoon olive oil

Pinch of red pepper flakes

½ teaspoon chopped fresh basil

Lightly chop the prosciutto and toss in oil and red pepper flakes; add basil.

ASSEMBLY:

Split each cupcake in half horizontally, spread ½ teaspoon hummus on the bottom half, and top with one portion of marinated prosciutto. Place the top of the muffin on prosciutto, and skewer the halves together.

CHEF'S NOTES:

The cupcakes can be lightly warmed, which will give a crisp texture that complements the hummus and prosciutto.

VARIATIONS:

Pulled pork or short ribs would also work well.

BEST SEASON:

Serve in spring and summer with a light Chardonnay or a Pinot Grigio.

GRILLED PORK SLAB SKEWERED WITH ROASTED JALAPEÑO AND BACON-BRAISED BRUSSELS SPROUTS

I always like to play with contrasting textures and flavors. Grilling the pork slab creates a crust on the outside while the inside remains tender. The crispy pork is a perfect vehicle for the roasted and braised vegetables. When you roast chiles, the natural sugars are concentrated and come forward in the bite; braising the sprouts with bacon infuses a rich, smoky flavor.

EXPERIENCE LEVEL: ②
YIELD: 12–16 BITES

PORK SLAB

2 pounds pork slab
1 cup olive oil
½ cup honey
1 teaspoon red pepper flakes
Salt and cracked black pepper to taste
Juice of 1 lime

Cut the pork slab into 2-inch pieces. Combine all the remaining ingredients, and toss the pork slab into the mixture. Allow the pork to sit in the mixture at least 1 hour at room temperature.

Prepare a grill.

Grill pork over medium heat on both sides until cooked through, about 5–7 minutes each side (internal temperature of 155°F). Keep on medium heat or meat will not char. Reserve for skewering.

ROASTED JALAPEÑOS

2 jalapeño chile peppers
½ teaspoon chili oil
Salt and pepper to taste
1 lime, for garnish

Prepare a grill.

Toss jalapeños in oil and season with salt and pepper. Grill over medium heat until all sides are brown. Remove from the grill and place in a paper bag until peppers are cooled. Slit them open, shake out the seeds, and cut the peppers into 1-inch squares. Reserve for assembly.

BACON-BRAISED BRUSSELS SPROUTS

6 large brussels sprouts
½ pound bacon, chopped
½ cup bacon fat
1 red onion, peeled and chopped

Trim the stem ends and cut the brussels sprouts into quarters. Heat a sauté pan over low heat; add the bacon and the bacon fat, and render until bacon is crisp. Add the red onion and cook until softened. Add brussels sprouts and cook for 10 minutes or until tender. Remove and hold at room temperature.

ASSEMBLY:

Cut lime into slices and place on serving board or plate. Take 2 brussels sprout quarters and skewer them (I use skewers from Pick On Us). Add a piece of jalapeño and then a piece of pork slab. Repeat until all ingredients are used. Serve immediately.

CHEF'S NOTES:

All items can be prepared a day ahead of time and stored, covered, in the refrigerator. Reheat and serve the next day.

VARIATIONS:

You can use braised short ribs as a tasty option. Use a habanero pepper (for more heat) or mushrooms instead of brussels sprouts.

BEST SEASON:

Fall is perfect for this dish; serve with a Pinot Noir or a pale ale.

JALAPEÑO PORK SLAB WITH BACON JAM

Chile-infused pork belly is flawlessly balanced by sweet and smoky bacon jam. This intense flavor combination will make your taste buds dance.

EXPERIENCE LEVEL: ②
YIELD: 8–10 BITES

JALAPEÑO PORK SLAB

3 jalapeño peppers, split, seeds removed, and chopped
2 teaspoons chili powder
½ teaspoon brown sugar
1 teaspoon olive oil
2 pounds pork slab
Rosemary, pea shoots, or any greens, for garnish

Combine jalapeños, chili powder, brown sugar, and oil to form a rub. Rub onto pork slab.

Prepare a grill.

Grill pork over medium heat on both sides until cooked through, about 5–7 minutes each side (internal temperature of 155°F). Keep on medium heat or the pork won't char. Let rest for 3–4 minutes before slicing into ¼-inch pieces.

CRISPY BRUSSELS SPROUTS

2 teaspoons olive oil
6 large brussels sprouts
Salt and pepper to taste

Core brussels sprouts and separate into leaves. Heat a sauté pan over high heat. Add oil, brussels sprout leaves, and salt and pepper to taste. Sauté until leaves are light brown and crisp.

BACON JAM

2 red onions, cut into small dice
1 cup honey
1 cup small-chopped bacon
1 teaspoon red pepper flakes

Combine all ingredients in a saucepan. Cook over low heat 15–20 minutes, stirring constantly.

ASSEMBLY:

In the bottom of a small cup or cone, place ½ teaspoon bacon jam, followed by 2 pieces of pork and small portion of brussels sprouts. Top with a little more jam from tip of teaspoon and garnish with rosemary, pea shoots, or any greens.

CHEF'S NOTES:

These items can be prepared ahead of time and finished just before serving. The bacon jam can be made a few days ahead of time and refrigerated.

VARIATIONS:

Use veal or chicken for this dish.

BEST SEASON:

Fall and winter are best for this dish. Serve with a Pinot Noir or an IPA.

BEER-BRAISED PORK SLAB, JALAPEÑO, AND CRISPY BRUSSELS SPROUT LEAVES ·

Rich and delicate, this braised pork slab bite calls for a bit of heat and crunch. When you sauté the leaves of brussels sprouts, they become chip-like.

EXPERIENCE LEVEL: ②
YIELD: 10–12 BITES

PORK SLAB

2 pounds pork slab

1 teaspoon ground cardamom

3 cups stout or other dark ale or beer

1 cup pork or chicken stock

Heat a heavy saucepan and sear the pork slab. Add cardamom, beer, and stock, covering the slab. Bring the liquids to a boil, then reduce to a simmer, cover, and cook for 20 minutes, or until pork is tender.

CRISPY BRUSSELS SPROUTS

2 teaspoons olive oil

6 large brussels sprouts

Salt and pepper to taste

Core brussels sprouts and separate into leaves. Heat a sauté pan over high heat. Add oil, brussels sprout leaves, and salt and pepper to taste. Sauté until leaves are light brown and crisp.

JALAPEÑOS

2 jalapeño peppers

2 teaspoons olive oil

Salt and pepper to taste

Preheat the oven to 350°F.

Toss jalapeños in oil and season with salt and pepper. Roast 20 minutes or until skin starts to blacken and pull from the flesh. Remove from oven and let cool. Split the peppers and remove the seeds. Cut jalapeños into 1-inch squares.

ASSEMBLY:

Slice the pork slab into ½-inch cubes. Place one piece on a spoon, top with a square of jalapeño, and follow with another piece of pork. Top the second piece with crisp brussels sprout leaves.

CHEF'S NOTES:

Ingredients can be prepared a day ahead—except for the brussels sprouts, which will not stay crispy. These need to be prepared shortly before serving.

VARIATIONS:

This can be made with chicken, beef short rib, or veal.

BEST SEASON:

This is a perfect dish for the fall and winter.

MID BITES

Snacks and Fillers for Platters, Bowls, Bigger Vessels, and Tabletop Snacks

Between that small and big bite comes the mid bite—the halfway point in the world of dining. It's a moment in culinary time that's often overlooked by home chefs, but not here! Now is the perfect time to add the mid bite to your culinary repertoire.

Beyond the bite-size appetizer are these two-or-three-bite dishes that, when presented together, offer your guests a variety of tastes and textures that can stand alone as the evening's fare or tease the palate for the big bites that lie ahead.

When creating recipes, I consider more than just how the flavors will come together. I think about how to take a traditional dish and turn it into something new without changing its foundation. For example, I love a cheese course—the mix of smooth and salty cheeses with the sweetness of a fruit. But instead of a hunk of cheddar with a bunch of grapes, try a "truffle" of blue and cream cheeses blended with crushed figs, surrounding a juicy grape center.

Mid bites are fun intermezzos of soups, salads, cheeses, dips, and more that offer classic party fare with a whole new twist. I love to lay out a number of mid bites on different serving vessels—platters, wood planks, silver trays, and antique tureens—just about anything that can hold the food. Remember, when two or more mid bites are brought together, there is love.

GOAT CHEESE, GRAPE, AND WALNUT ROULADE

The roulade is a fun way to incorporate many flavors into one bite. The burst of the grapes, the smoothness of the goat cheese, and the crunch of the walnuts make the texture and experience one of a kind.

EXPERIENCE LEVEL: ①
YIELD: 8–10 SERVINGS

1 quart seedless grapes, any variety

Small handful of fresh thyme leaves

1–2 tablespoons extra-virgin olive oil

Sea salt to taste

Black pepper to taste

10 walnut halves, rough chopped

1 pound Joan of Arc Goat Cheese with Garlic & Herbs (or other quality goat cheese)

2 tablespoons honey

Preheat the oven to 375°F. Scatter the grapes on a small baking sheet with most of the thyme, a little olive oil, salt, and pepper, and shake to coat them. Roast in the oven until the grapes start to blister and color, 10–15 minutes. Coat the walnuts with a little olive oil and roast on another small baking sheet until fragrant and toasted, 5–6 minutes. Cool both the grapes and walnuts.

In a small mixing bowl combine goat cheese and walnuts. Mix until fully incorporated, soft, and smooth. Lay a 12 × 12-inch piece of plastic wrap on a work surface. Spread the goat cheese onto the plastic, forming a bed approximately 8 inches square.

Lightly chop the grapes. Gently press the chopped grapes into the goat cheese. Lift the plastic wrap, pulling the closest edge up and forcing the goat cheese to roll and form a roulade. Tighten the plastic around it and store the roulade in the refrigerator until firm, about 1 hour. Serve with crackers or a toasted baguette.

CHEF'S NOTES:

This may be made up to 2 days in advance.

VARIATIONS:

You can use pecans instead of walnuts and dried cranberries instead of grapes.

BEST SEASON:

Year-round.

GOAT CHEESE, GRAPE, AND WALNUT SPREAD

The combination of fruit and cheese has always been a staple in every traditional kitchen. By adding the citrus zest to this dish you have taken a step into the culinary wow zone. This is a spread that has complex flavors, fruit undertones, and a hint of earthiness from the walnuts. Sit back and enjoy this spread and transport your palate to a happy place.

EXPERIENCE LEVEL: ①
YIELD: 8–10 SERVINGS

2 cups walnuts, divided

¾ cup honey

1 cup sliced red grapes

2 teaspoons herbes de Provence

1 teaspoon ground coriander

2 tablespoons finely grated orange zest

1 tablespoon fresh-squeezed orange juice

1 teaspoon fresh-squeezed lemon juice

⅛ teaspoon salt

4 ounces Joan of Arc Natural Flavor Goat Cheese
   (or other quality goat cheese), softened

Coarsely chop 1 cup walnuts; chop the remaining cup of walnuts finely. Place finely chopped nuts in a large bowl and add the honey, ¾ cup sliced grapes, herbes de Provence, coriander, orange zest, orange juice, lemon juice, and salt. Slowly mix until all ingredients are incorporated.

Line an 8-to-10-ounce soufflé cup with plastic wrap.

Soften goat cheese to a spreadable point. Use a piping bag or spoon, fill the bottom ½ inch of the plastic-lined soufflé cup (this will be the top) with the goat cheese. Add ½ cup of the rough-chop walnuts. Sprinkle half the remaining sliced grapes over the goat cheese. Pipe or spoon more goat cheese on top of the grapes, covering them completely. Spoon in about ½ inch of the walnut-grape mixture. Repeat with a layer of goat cheese, the remaining grapes, the remaining rough-chop walnuts, and a final layer of goat cheese (this will be the bottom). Fold the plastic over the contents of the soufflé cup. Refrigerate overnight.

When you are ready to use the spread, open the plastic wrap and invert a plate over the soufflé cup. Turn the soufflé cup over, separating it from the goat cheese spread. Serve with crackers or bread.

CHEF'S NOTES:

This can be made up to 2 days ahead, stored in the refrigerator. Delicious with a toasted baguette.

VARIATIONS:

Substitute Port Salut or Roquefort cheese for a more intense flavor.

BEST SEASON:

All year.

SALMON DILL HORSERADISH SPREAD WITH HERB CROSTINI

The classic combination of fresh dill and smoked salmon is kicked up a notch with the heat of the fiery horseradish root. In addition to herb crostini, this can be served with bagel crisps, flatbreads, or chips.

EXPERIENCE LEVEL: ②
YIELD: 6–8 SERVINGS

SALMON SPREAD

16 ounces cream cheese, softened
12 ounces smoked salmon, chopped
3 dashes Worcestershire sauce
3 tablespoons prepared horseradish
3 drops hot pepper sauce
1 teaspoon chopped fresh dill weed
2 tablespoons chopped scallions

In a medium bowl, stir cream cheese until it is no longer in a block. Add salmon, Worcestershire sauce, horseradish, hot pepper sauce, dill, and scallions; mix well. Pack the spread in a small dish and refrigerate until ready to serve.

HERB CROSTINI

¼ cup olive oil
¼ cup butter
2 tablespoons finely chopped Italian parsley
2 cloves garlic, minced
Salt and pepper to taste
1 French baguette, cut diagonally into ½-inch slices
¼ cup grated Parmesan cheese

Set the oven to broil. In a small saucepan, combine the olive oil, butter, parsley, and garlic. Set the pan over medium heat until the butter has melted and the mixture starts to bubble. Season with salt and pepper. Remove from the heat. Dip each slice of bread into the garlic mixture, turning to coat each side. Place Parmesan cheese on a plate. Press one side of each piece of bread into the cheese, and place the bread, cheese side up, on a baking sheet. Broil on the middle rack of the preheated oven for about 8 minutes, or until golden brown.

CHEF'S NOTES:

This spread can be made a few days in advance. Be sure to cover tightly, because the spread will pick up any odors from the refrigerator.

VARIATIONS:

This can be made with trout, whitefish, or even chicken as an option.

BEST SEASON:

This dish is perfect for a light spring or summer Sunday brunch with friends and family. Serve with a Pinot Grigio, Chardonnay, or a light ale.

SALMON DILL HORSERADISH BAGEL-DUST CUP

I like to make "dusts" out of ordinary ingredients to impart a different texture to a familiar flavor. Layer smoked salmon with dill, horseradish cream, and bagel dust in a glass to create a twisted bagel and lox for your brunch buffet.

EXPERIENCE LEVEL: ②
YIELD: 6–8 SERVINGS

SMOKED SALMON SALAD

1 pound smoked salmon
1 tablespoon chopped fresh dill

Roughly chop salmon and toss in dill.

HORSERADISH CREAM

¼ cup mayonnaise
½ cup prepared horseradish
2 tablespoons Dijon mustard
¾ cup heavy cream, whipped to soft peaks
Pinch of white sugar, or to taste
Salt and black pepper to taste

Stir the mayonnaise, horseradish, and Dijon mustard in a bowl until evenly combined. Fold in the whipped cream, then season to taste with sugar, salt, and pepper. Refrigerate until ready to assemble.

BAGEL DUST

1 plain bagel
1 tablespoon chopped fresh dill
Salt and pepper to taste

Preheat the oven to 250°F.

Cut the bagel into small chunks. Place on a sheet pan; sprinkle with chopped dill, salt, and pepper; and cook until toasted and dried, about 15 minutes. Remove bagel from the oven and let cool, then place in the food processor and grind to a dust.

ASSEMBLY:

Layer salmon-dill salad, horseradish cream, and bagel dust in glasses.

CHEF'S NOTES:
Bagel dust can be made a few days ahead. Store in an airtight container at room temperature.

You can assemble this bite a few hours before serving, but not too much earlier or the horseradish cream will soften the dust and make it soggy.

VARIATIONS:
Use smoked sable, smoked whitefish, smoked scallops, or shrimp as a variation.

BEST SEASON:
This is best for summer brunch, or even as a fun starter for lunch.

STRAWBERRY, GOAT CHEESE, AND LEEK TART

This tart is delicious warm, but it is very versatile and can be served at room temperature as well. Pair it with a salad for a light plated lunch, or feature it on your breakfast or brunch buffet.

EXPERIENCE LEVEL: ③
YIELD: 6 SERVINGS

Pastry for a 12 x 3-inch rectangular tart pan

5 leeks, split, well washed, and julienned

2 tablespoons olive oil

Salt and pepper to taste

8 egg yolks

2 cups heavy whipping cream

4½ ounces Joan of Arc Goat Cheese Log
   with Peppadew

8 strawberries, hulled and diced

Preheat the oven to 400°F. Fit the pastry into a 12 x 3-inch fluted tart pan with a removable bottom. Chill for 15 minutes. Line with foil and fill with pie weights. Bake for 10 minutes. Remove foil and weights, and bake for another 5 minutes.

Put julienned leeks in a roasting tin, drizzle with oil, and season with salt and pepper. Roast for 15 minutes. Set aside to cool.

Reduce oven temperature to 375°F.

Beat together egg yolks and cream, and season with salt and pepper. Arrange the leeks over the base of the baked pastry. Pour cream mixture over leeks. Slice the goat cheese thinly, and dot over the top of the tart. Sprinkle with strawberries and bake for 30 minutes, or until custard has just set. Cut into 2-inch strips and serve.

CHEF'S NOTES:
This is best made just before serving; however, you can prepare it the day before as long as you reheat it slowly to an internal temperature of 145°F.

VARIATIONS:
Change the leeks to red onions, goat cheese to Roquefort cheese, and strawberries to blueberries.

BEST SEASON:
This is great for an end-of-summer breakfast or brunch; serve with a light white wine or pale ale.

GOAT CHEESE, STRAWBERRY, AND LEEK TRUFFLE

Hands down, one of my favorite pairings is ripe strawberries with creamy, tangy fresh goat cheese. Here they are rolled together with sweet spring leeks into a "truffle" that your guests can just pop in their mouths. The really fun twist is that the strawberries and leeks are oven dried to concentrate the sugars and create a crust for the goat cheese balls.

EXPERIENCE LEVEL: ②
YIELD: 12–16 PIECES

8 ounces Joan of Arc Natural Flavor Goat Cheese (or other quality goat cheese), softened

4 ounces cream cheese, softened

2 leeks, white and light green parts only, well washed and finely diced

1 cup thinly sliced strawberries

Salt and pepper to taste

Combine goat cheese and cream cheese in a bowl, mix well to blend, cover, and place in the refrigerator. Once mixture hardens, scoop out generous tablespoons and roll into balls. Return to refrigerator, covered, until ready to use.

Preheat the oven to 120°F.

Dry the diced leeks on a sheet pan placed in the preheated oven for 1 hour. On a separate sheet pan, dry the strawberries for 2 hours. These may be in the oven together but must be in separate pans, or the moisture from the strawberries will affect the leeks. Remove strawberries and leeks from oven, being sure they are dried; they should be crisp like a potato chip. Lightly chop both leeks and strawberries separately.

Combine the dried strawberries and leeks on a sheet pan. Remove goat cheese "truffles" from refrigerator and roll lightly in the chopped dried strawberry and leeks.

CHEF'S NOTES:

The uncoated goat-cheese balls can be made several days in advance and refrigerated in an airtight container. The strawberries and leeks can also be oven dried in advance as long as they are kept in separate airtight containers in a cool, dry place.

VARIATIONS:

Change goat cheese to another soft cheese such as Cotswold or Gorgonzola.

BEST SEASON:

This dish is best served in the spring or summer, as part of a brunch buffet or on a fruit and cheese platter.

CHORIZO DOUGHNUTS

I like to transform a typically sweet item into a savory dish. Fried spicy pork . . . need I say more?

EXPERIENCE LEVEL: ②
YIELD: 14–16 BITES

SAUTÉED PEPPERS

2 red peppers

½ cup olive oil

½ cup tomato sauce

½ cup sugar

½ cup Alessi Red Wine Vinegar
   (or any quality red wine vinegar)

Split peppers in half, seed, and julienne them. Heat the oil in a sauté pan, add red peppers, and sauté until slightly soft. Add tomato sauce, sugar, and vinegar. Cook for 20 minutes or until peppers are soft. Let cool. Once peppers are cooled, chop into small pieces and reserve.

DOUGHNUTS

5 tablespoons white sugar, divided

1 tablespoon active dry yeast

¼ cup vegetable oil

1 tablespoon fresh-squeezed lemon juice

1 teaspoon salt

4 cups all-purpose flour

4 cups whole wheat flour

1 pound chorizo sausage, cooked, cooled, and
   chopped roughly

2 quarts canola oil for frying

Dissolve 1 tablespoon sugar and yeast in ½ cup warm water (110°F). Set aside until foamy.

In a large bowl, mix together oil, lemon juice, 2⅓ cups warm water (110°F), salt, and 4 tablespoons sugar. Add yeast mixture, and gradually mix in the flours. Place the dough in a buttered bowl, and turn to coat. Cover with a damp tea towel and leave in a warm place to rise for 1½ hours. Mix in the cooked chorizo. Form dough into balls about the size of an egg and flatten them into 2-inch rounds, pushing your finger through the center to make a hole.

Heat oil to 350°F in a 4-quart pot. Fry the doughnuts one at a time, until light brown on both sides. Place on paper towels to drain.

Serve the doughnuts warm or room temperature with sautéed peppers.

CHEF'S NOTES:

This is a great addition to a brunch or early dinner.

VARIATIONS:

Add different seasonings such as cracked black pepper, Cajun seasoning, or barbecue seasoning to create a different flavor profile. Or use Italian sausage for another taste.

BEST SEASON:

This item can be served on a summer evening or a fall afternoon. It goes great with a Spanish wine.

CHORIZO EMPANADA

These Portuguese pocket pies are addictive! They were first created to allow workers to easily transport a hearty meal. Try them with cooling guacamole, salsa, and sour cream for dipping.

EXPERIENCE LEVEL: ③
YIELD: 16–18 BITES

4½ cups all-purpose flour

1½ teaspoons salt, plus a pinch

½ cup shortening

1¼ cups water, or as needed

2 tablespoons olive oil

1 small onion, chopped

1½ pounds ground chorizo

2 tablespoons paprika

1 teaspoon ground cumin

½ teaspoon freshly ground black pepper

½ cup raisins

1 tablespoon Alessi Italian White Wine Vinegar
   (or other quality white wine vinegar)

2 hard-cooked eggs, peeled and chopped

1 quart oil for frying, or as needed

In a medium bowl, stir together the flour and 1½ teaspoons salt. Cut in shortening using a pastry blender, or pinch it into small pieces using your fingers, until the mixture resembles coarse crumbs. Use a fork to stir in water a few tablespoons at a time, just until the mixture forms a ball. Pat the mixture into a smooth ball and flatten slightly. Wrap in plastic wrap and refrigerate for 1 hour.

Heat the olive oil in a large skillet over medium heat. Add the onion and cook until tender. Crumble in the chorizo, and season with paprika, cumin, black pepper, and a pinch of salt. Cook, stirring frequently, until the chorizo is browned. Drain excess grease, and stir in the raisins and vinegar. Refrigerate until chilled. Stir in the hard-cooked eggs.

Form the dough into 2-inch balls. On a floured surface, roll each ball out into a thin circle. Spoon some of the meat mixture onto the center, then fold the round into a half-moon shape. Seal the edges by pressing with your fingers or a fork, using a bit of water if needed.

Heat the oil in a deep-fryer to 365°F. Place one or two pies in the fryer at a time. Cook for about 5 minutes, turning once to brown both sides. Drain on paper towels, and serve hot.

CHEF'S NOTES:

Empanadas can be made ahead of time and frozen before frying.

These are delicious served with your favorite salsa, sour cream, and guacamole.

VARIATIONS:

Use ground beef or ground Italian sausage instead of chorizo.

BEST SEASON:

This dish can be made year-round.

KALAMATA OLIVE HUMMUS

Kalamata olives are often referred to as the Greek olive. They add meatiness and a salty kick to basic hummus. Enjoy this nosh with flatbreads and a Spanish Rioja or fruity Provençal rosé.

EXPERIENCE LEVEL: ①
YIELD: 6–8 SERVINGS

1 clove garlic, peeled
1 cup garbanzo beans, liquid reserved
1 cup kalamata olives, pitted
4 tablespoons lemon juice
2 tablespoons tahini
1 teaspoon salt
Black pepper to taste
2 tablespoons olive oil

Chop the garlic in a blender. Pour the garbanzo beans and olives into blender, reserving about a tablespoon of olives for garnish. Place lemon juice, tahini, and salt in the blender. Blend until creamy and well mixed, adding small amounts of reserved bean liquid until smooth. Transfer the mixture to a medium serving bowl. Sprinkle with pepper and pour olive oil over the top. Garnish with the reserved olives.

CHEF'S NOTES:

This can be made days ahead. The flavors will develop as it sits.

VARIATIONS:

You can substitute sun-dried tomato, white bean garlic, or other type of flavoring for the olives. Just be sure to take into consideration the water content of anything you use.

BEST SEASON:

All year.

ROASTED VEGETABLE HUMMUS

Roasting vegetables brings out their natural sweetness. Here they mingle with notes of cumin and cayenne, and when they're folded into lemony hummus, the flavors balance each other, creating harmony in every bite.

EXPERIENCE LEVEL: ②
YIELD: 8–10 SERVINGS

1 small eggplant, cut into 1-inch cubes

1 red bell pepper, seeded and cut into 1-inch pieces

1 red onion, peeled and cut into 1-inch pieces

2 plum tomatoes, seeded and quartered

5–6 tablespoons olive oil, divided

2 teaspoons salt, divided, plus more to taste

1 cup cooked garbanzo beans, drained if using canned beans

3 garlic cloves, peeled and chopped

½ cup tahini

3 teaspoons ground cumin

3 tablespoons kalamata olives, pitted

¼ teaspoon cayenne pepper, or more (or less) to taste

Vegetable broth for thinning (optional)

Pepper to taste

Preheat the oven to 400°F. Toss the eggplant, bell pepper, onion, and tomatoes in a bowl with 1 tablespoon olive oil and ½ teaspoon salt. Spread them in one layer on a baking sheet and roast 30–40 minutes, until the vegetables are very lightly browned and soft. Cool slightly.

In a food processor, place garbanzo beans, garlic, tahini, and 4 tablespoons olive oil. Process until the beans and garlic are almost completely ground. Add roasted vegetables to the processor along with the cumin, olives, remaining 1½ teaspoons salt, and cayenne pepper. You can add more or less cayenne to suit your family's taste buds; I usually add at least another ¼ teaspoon to ours. Process until almost smooth, leaving some texture and small bits of the roasted vegetables and olives showing through. Add more olive oil or some vegetable broth if you want to thin it out a bit. Taste for salt and pepper. Serve at room temperature with pita bread.

CHEF'S NOTES:

This item can be made a few days ahead. I have found that the flavors continue to develop as time goes by.

VARIATIONS:

Using edamame or sweet peas as the base instead of chickpeas creates a different flavor altogether.

BEST SEASON:

This is a great early-summer item; serve with a light Chardonnay or light IPA.

FIG, ROQUEFORT, AND GRAPE TRUFFLES

When you bite into this sweet and savory Roquefort cheese "truffle," you experience a burst of sweet juice from the red grape nestled inside. Your party guests will be talking about this creation at the office on Monday.

EXPERIENCE LEVEL: ①
YIELD: 24 BITES

½ pound cream cheese, softened

1 pound Joan of Arc Roquefort cheese (or any quality Roquefort cheese), softened

½ pound Joan of Arc Goat Cheese with Fig, softened

24 red grapes

2 teaspoons honey

Combine cream cheese, Roquefort cheese, and fig-goat cheese in a mixing bowl and blend well until smooth. Divide mixture into 1-ounce pieces about the size of a large marble. Take a grape and punch it into the middle of the cheese mixture, rolling to cover and forming it into balls.

Drizzle honey over the cheese balls and skewer before serving (I use skewers from Pick On Us).

CHEF'S NOTES:

These can be made one day ahead of time, covered, and refrigerated. If you can't find goat cheese with figs, use plain goat cheese with 10 dried figs, finely chopped.

VARIATIONS:

Instead of Roquefort cheese you can use traditional blue cheese, goat cheese, or port-wine cheese.

BEST SEASON:

This is a great item for fall and winter; serve with a nice Meritage or pale ale.

FIG, ROQUEFORT, GOAT CHEESE, AND GRAPE SPREAD

This spread is easy and quick to assemble for a last-minute get-together. It will enhance any cheese or meat board and can also serve as an after-dinner cheese course paired with an aged port or Sauternes.

EXPERIENCE LEVEL: ①
YIELD: 8–10 SERVINGS

1 pound Joan of Arc Roquefort cheese (or any quality Roquefort), softened
½ pound Joan of Arc Goat Cheese with Fig (or any quality goat cheese), softened
½ pound cream cheese, softened
½ cup red grapes, sliced
½ cup dried figs, quartered

Combine the cheeses in a mixer bowl and mix on medium speed until thoroughly incorporated. Using a rubber spatula, slowly incorporate the sliced grapes and dried figs into the mixture. Scoop into a ramekin or bowl and serve with crostini or crackers.

CHEF'S NOTES:

This can be made a day ahead, covered, and refrigerated until serving. It can also be heated gently and served warm.

VARIATIONS:

Eliminate the goat cheese to intensify the flavor of the Roquefort.

BEST SEASON:

Serve in the late summer or early fall with a Cabernet Sauvignon or an IPA.

CARROT, CRAB, AND ORANGE SOUP

The combination of carrot and orange is a hidden treasure to most, but add the flavor of crab and you are transported to a light summer day on the shore. Enjoy this easy, delicious, and flavorful soup that has levels of both flavor and character.

EXPERIENCE LEVEL: ②
YIELD: 4–6 SERVINGS

1 large onion

8 medium-large carrots

Small piece of butter

1 tablespoon olive oil

1 orange

4 cups vegetable stock

Black pepper to taste (optional)

Fresh cilantro, chopped (optional)

½ pound jumbo lump crabmeat

1 leek, well washed and thinly sliced, for
     garnish (optional)

Peel onion and cut in half lengthwise. Place halves, cut side down, on a chopping board and cut each into thin strips. Peel the carrots and cut the ends off. Slice each carrot in half crosswise, then lengthwise. Place on chopping board with flat sides down, and dice into ¼-inch pieces. Put the butter and oil in a saucepan over low heat, add sliced onion, and cook for 10 minutes, stirring regularly.

Using a cheese grater, grate the zest from the orange into a small bowl. Add the zest and the carrots to the pan with the onion. Cover and cook for 10 more minutes, stirring occasionally. Add the stock and bring up to a simmer, then put the lid back on the pan and simmer gently. After 45 minutes, test the carrots by poking them with a knife or skewer. If they are soft enough, turn off the heat.

Carefully ladle the very hot soup into a food processor. Puree the soup until it is smooth. Cut the orange in half, remove any visible pips, and squeeze the juice from one half through a strainer into the soup. Return the soup to the pan, heat it gently, and taste. (Careful, it's hot!) You might like to add a grinding of black pepper or a little chopped fresh cilantro. Serve soup, adding crabmeat 1 teaspoon at a time so it stays whole. Garnish with a few orange segments and a few rings of thinly sliced leeks, if desired.

CHEF'S NOTES:
The soup is delicious cold in place of a summer gazpacho. Try tangerines or blood oranges for a change in flavor.

VARIATIONS:
The same recipe concept can be used for beets, sweet potatoes, or corn in place of the carrots.

BEST SEASON:
Serve hot in fall or chilled for spring or summer.

CARROT, CRAB, AND ORANGE SALAD

This salad makes a lovely first course or entree for a light summer luncheon, with carrots and oranges adding crunch and color to a green salad, while sweet crabmeat balances the acid in the citrus and adds textural diversity.

EXPERIENCE LEVEL: ①
YIELD: 4–6 SERVINGS

ORANGE VINAIGRETTE

2 medium oranges, zested and juiced
2 tablespoons Alessi Balsamic Vinegar (or any quality balsamic vinegar)
2 tablespoons honey
1 clove garlic, peeled
¾ teaspoon salt
¾ teaspoon freshly ground black pepper
¾ cup extra-virgin olive oil

In a blender, combine the orange zest, orange juice, balsamic vinegar, honey, garlic, salt, and pepper. Blend until smooth. With the blender running, add the olive oil in a steady stream until combined. Transfer to a container and store in the refrigerator.

SALAD

2 heads Bibb lettuce
3 oranges, peeled and segmented
1 large beet, cooked, peeled, and diced
1 large carrot, peeled and julienned
½ pound jumbo lump crabmeat
1 leek, sliced into thin rings, blanched in hot water, and chilled

ASSEMBLY:

Lay Bibb lettuce leaves on a large plate, sprinkle with orange segments, beets, and carrots, then top with crabmeat. Drizzle generously with vinaigrette and top with leek rings.

CHEF'S NOTES:

The dressing can be made a few days ahead, and the beet can be cooked and diced a day ahead.

VARIATIONS:

Instead of beets, try pomegranate; instead of crab, use shrimp. Both create a completely different experience.

BEST SEASON:

Summer is the best time for this dish; serve with a light Chardonnay or a Pinot Grigio.

PORTOBELLO, PANCETTA, AND MASCARPONE SPREAD WITH BACON CRISPS

Mild mascarpone cheese is the perfect accompaniment to porto-bello mushrooms; it will not overpower the earthy flavor of the mushrooms. Using both pancetta and bacon allows the flavors to build from salty to smoky, complementing the essence of umami.

EXPERIENCE LEVEL: ②
YIELD: 6–8 SERVINGS

2 cups white wine (preferably Chardonnay)

4–6 ounces dried portobello mushrooms

½ cup pancetta, diced

8 ounces mascarpone cheese

1 teaspoon dried tarragon

8 ounces cream cheese, cut into cubes

½ cup sour cream

1 teaspoon salt

½ teaspoon freshly ground black pepper

½ pound bacon, cooked crisp and left whole, for garnish

Heat wine in a saucepan. Remove from the heat, place dried mushrooms in wine, and let sit for 10 minutes to rehydrate. Transfer mushrooms with ⅔ cup of the liquid to a food processor. Puree to a coarse consistency.

Heat a nonstick pan over medium heat and add pancetta—do not mix, toss, or stir; allow the pancetta to crisp. Once crisp, remove it to a paper towel to remove excess oil.

In a medium pot combine remaining ingredients (except the bacon) and the pureed mushrooms. Mix thoroughly and cook over medium-low heat 5–10 minutes, stirring frequently; add pancetta. Transfer to a bowl and let cool.

ASSEMBLY:

In individual small bowls or mason jars, place 3 tablespoons mushroom mixture. Insert a piece of bacon upright or lay it decoratively across the top and serve.

CHEF'S NOTES:

This can be made a day or so in advance. Serve with naan bread, pita chips, or crostini.

VARIATIONS:

You can increase the amount of cream cheese.

BEST SEASON:

This can be made year-round.

PORTOBELLO, PANCETTA, AND MASCARPONE SOUP

There are few things as comforting as creamy mushroom soup. Sweet mascarpone heightens the richness and gives this soup a luxurious texture, and pancetta crisps lend a subtle and inviting saltiness to each bite.

EXPERIENCE LEVEL: ①
YIELD: 6–8 SERVINGS

4 tablespoons unsalted butter, divided

8 ounces pancetta, diced

4 leeks (white and light green parts only), well washed and thinly sliced

Salt and freshly ground pepper to taste

2 (5-inch) portobello mushroom caps, stemmed and chopped

3 tablespoons all-purpose flour

2 tablespoons sherry (optional)

2 cups low-sodium chicken broth

½ cup half-and-half

4 ounces mascarpone

4 ounces Joan of Arc Goat Cheese with Garlic & Herbs

Melt 2 tablespoons butter in a saucepan over medium-high heat. Add the pancetta and cook until browned, 5–8 minutes. Remove with a slotted spoon to a plate. To the saucepan, add ½ tablespoon butter, 1 cup of the leeks, and salt and pepper to taste. Cook 4 minutes, then remove to the plate; set aside.

Add the remaining 1½ tablespoons butter, leeks, ½ teaspoon salt, and pepper to taste to the pan; cook until wilted, about 3 minutes. Add the mushrooms and cook 3 minutes. Sprinkle in the flour and cook, stirring constantly, 2 minutes. If desired, stir in 2 tablespoons sherry, scraping up any browned bits with a wooden spoon and cooking until the sherry evaporates. Add the broth and 2 cups water. Cover and bring to a boil, then reduce the heat to low and simmer, uncovered, until the mushrooms are tender, 8–10 minutes.

Puree the soup in batches in a blender until smooth. Return to the pot, whisk in the half-and-half, mascarpone, and goat cheese, and bring just to below a boil. Stir in three-quarters of the pancetta-leek mixture, then portion the soup into bowls, topping it with a bit of the remaining pancetta-leek mixture.

CHEF'S NOTES:

This dish can be made ahead of time and reheated when need. It can also be frozen for up to a month in a sealed airtight container.

VARIATIONS:

Change up the dish by adding grilled chicken.

Instead of pancetta, you can also use ham or bacon.

BEST SEASON:

This dish is best served during the cold fall and winter months.

BUTTERNUT SQUASH DIP

When the leaves begin to change color in the fall, I can't wait for late harvest vegetables. Earthy and sweet butternut squash makes a vibrant and delicate warm dip for various breads and crisps.

EXPERIENCE LEVEL: ①
YIELD: 4–6 SERVINGS

1 medium butternut squash, halved and seeded
3 tablespoons olive oil
1 whole head garlic
11 ounces Joan of Arc Natural Flavor Goat Cheese
    (or any quality goat cheese), softened
Juice of 1 lemon
Salt and pepper to taste

Preheat the oven to 350°F.

Brush the cut side of the squash halves with some of the olive oil and place them on a baking sheet, oiled side down. Cut the top off the head of garlic and drizzle the remaining olive oil over it. Wrap the garlic in aluminum foil and place it on the baking sheet with the squash. Bake for about 40 minutes, or until the squash can easily be pierced with a fork. Scoop the squash out of its skin and into a mixing bowl, reserving a small portion for garnish, if desired. Squeeze the cloves of garlic out of their skins and into the bowl with the squash. Mash until smooth. Stir in the goat cheese and lemon juice until well blended. Season with salt and pepper to taste. Transfer to a serving bowl. Serve warm or at room temperature.

CHEF'S NOTES:

Serve this dish with pita chips, lavash crisps, or grilled focaccia bread.

VARIATIONS:

For a fall flavor and vibe, add toasted, chopped nuts such as walnuts, chestnuts, or pecans.

BEST SEASON:

Fall or winter works best for this dish, as the flavors evoke the cool-weather seasons.

BUTTERNUT SQUASH SOUP

This flavorful squash soup is an enchanting way to celebrate autumn. As a first course, serve it warm in small bowls or passed in demitasse cups.

EXPERIENCE LEVEL: ①
YIELD: 8–10 SERVINGS

2 tablespoons unsalted butter
1 small onion, chopped
1 stalk celery, chopped
1 medium carrot, peeled and chopped
2 medium potatoes, peeled and cubed
1 medium butternut squash, peeled, seeded, and
    cubed
4 cups chicken stock
Salt and pepper to taste

Melt the butter in a large stockpot and cook the onion, celery, carrot, potatoes, and squash 5 minutes, or until lightly browned. Pour in enough chicken stock to cover vegetables. Bring to a boil. Reduce heat to low, cover pot, and simmer 40 minutes, or until all vegetables are tender. Transfer the soup to a blender, and blend until smooth. Return to pot, and mix in any remaining stock to attain desired consistency. Season with salt and pepper.

CHEF'S NOTES:

To make this soup vegan, use vegetable stock and replace the butter with oil.

This can also be made a few days ahead and reheated when needed.

VARIATIONS:

You can use acorn squash in place of the butternut squash.

Add a touch of roasted apples for a bit of fall sweetness and a different flavor.

BEST SEASON:

This soup is great for a fall or winter meal.

ROQUEFORT, HONEY, AND FIG CUSTARD

The slightly pungent Roquefort cheese offsets the sweetness and crunch of honeyed figs, creating this robust custard. Serve with crusty bread and watch it disappear.

EXPERIENCE LEVEL: ②
YIELD: 8 SERVINGS

1 cup heavy cream

½ cup crème fraîche

1 cup Joan of Arc Roquefort cheese (or any quality Roquefort), divided

Salt and pepper to taste

5 large eggs

2 tablespoons minced fresh chives

3 dried figs, quartered

Preheat the oven to 325°F, and bring a medium-size pot of water almost to a boil.

In the bowl of a stand mixer, combine the heavy cream, crème fraîche, and ½ cup Roquefort cheese. Using the whisk attachment, combine until smooth. Mix in salt and pepper to taste. Crack eggs into a separate small bowl and beat lightly. Slowly add the beaten eggs to the mixer bowl, add the chives, and combine well.

Place eight (2–3-ounce) ramekins in an ovenproof baking dish. Divide the custard equally among the ramekins and sprinkle the remaining ½ cup cheese into the centers of the custards. Gently pour the hot water into the baking dish until it comes halfway up the outsides of the ramekins. Cover the baking dish lightly with foil; make sure to leave the ends open so steam can escape. Bake the custards 30 minutes, rotating the pan in the oven after 15 minutes. The custards are done when there is no jiggle in the center and they are just beginning to puff. Remove from the oven, top each with a dried fig quarter, and serve warm or at room temperature.

CHEF'S NOTES:

The custard can be made a day ahead, but do not bake until the day of serving. Store the custard in the refrigerator, covered, until ready to bake.

VARIATIONS:

Substitute traditional blue cheese, Port Salut, or goat cheese for Roquefort. You can also cook in larger ramekins.

BEST SEASON:

Fall and winter.

ROQUEFORT-HONEY FIGS

With this presentation, the fig acts as a vessel housing its instinctive Roquefort-cheese partner. In one bite you encounter a burst of salty, sweet, savory, and earthy flavors in harmony with one another.

EXPERIENCE LEVEL: ①
YIELD: 24 BITES

3 ounces Joan of Arc Roquefort cheese
   (or any quality Roquefort)
12 dried figs, halved
12 red grapes, halved
2 teaspoons honey

Divide the cheese into small (¼-ounce) penny-size balls. Set aside.

With your fingertip, press an indentation into each fig half. Fill the fig with a ball of Roquefort, and lightly push a half grape into the cheese. Place each fig half on a spoon and drizzle with honey before serving.

CHEF'S NOTES:

Use fresh figs when in season instead of dried.

VARIATIONS:

For variety you can use goat cheese mixed with toasted pistachio nuts and drizzled with a balsamic reduction.

BEST SEASON:

This is a great fall item served warm.

TUNA CRUDO WITH NOODLE SALAD

Crudo is the Italian word for "raw." It's important to use the highest quality and freshest tuna. I like to experiment with building flavors that highlight the quality and pure taste of the fish rather than overpower it.

EXPERIENCE LEVEL: ③
YIELD: 8–10 SERVINGS

NOODLE SALAD

2 (8-ounce) packages dried soba noodles
1 zucchini, grated with a wide grater or peeled into thin strips with a vegetable peeler
1 tomato, seeded and cut into small pieces
1 red or green chile, seeded and thinly sliced
1 red bell pepper, seeded and cut into strips
1 green pepper, seeded and cut into strips
3 scallions, sliced
1 cup fresh cilantro, lightly chopped
½ cup chopped fresh basil

Cook noodles according to package directions. Drain and cool. Combine all remaining ingredients and mix well. Finish with enough sauce (recipe below) to lightly coat noodles.

NOODLE SAUCE

⅓ cup fresh-squeezed lime juice
4 tablespoons fish sauce
2 tablespoons soy sauce
2 teaspoons chili sauce
2 cloves garlic, minced
2 tablespoons sugar

Mix all dressing ingredients together in a cup or small bowl until sugar dissolves. Taste for sour/sweetness, adding more sugar as desired. Note that the taste of the dressing will be very "zingy" at this point because of the lime juice—it will taste milder when distributed among the noodles.

BANG BANG SAUCE

½ cup mayonnaise (preferably Hellman's)
¼ cup Thai sweet chili sauce
4–8 drops Sriracha sauce
1 teaspoon peanut butter
⅛ teaspoon garlic powder

Combine all ingredients and mix well. Reserve.

WASABI AIOLI

1 tablespoon prepared real wasabi paste
2 tablespoons minced garlic
1 tablespoon minced ginger
2 tablespoons rice vinegar
2 egg yolks*
1 cup canola oil
Salt and freshly ground black pepper to taste.

In a food processor, blend wasabi paste, garlic, ginger, vinegar, and egg yolks. While processor is running, drizzle in oil, slowly at first until it emulsifies, then more quickly.

Adjust seasoning.

*Eating undercooked eggs and raw fish is not healthy for some people.

TUNA CRUDO

1 pound highest quality tuna* (preferably a thick piece from the loin)

1 teaspoon salt

2 medium shallots, finely diced (about ¼ cup)

2 teaspoons capers, drained well and chopped

¼ teaspoon crushed red pepper flakes

12 leaves basil, thinly sliced

¼ cup olive oil

Juice of 1 lemon (at least 2 tablespoons)

Sprinkle tuna generously with salt, followed by the shallots, capers, red pepper flakes, and basil. Place tuna in the freezer for 10 minutes; this helps it firm up, which makes it easier to slice. Using a sharp chef's knife, cut the tuna into slices roughly ⅛-inch thick. As you work, gently press each slice onto the cutting surface with your fingers to flatten it, then transfer to a large platter.

Combine the olive oil and lemon juice in a sealable container, close the container, and shake well until the oil is emulsified. Spoon this vinaigrette over the fish. Serve immediately with noodle salad.

ASSEMBLY:

Divide noodles among 4–6 plates, placing them off to one side of each plate. Dot the center of the plate with three dots each of bang bang sauce and wasabi aioli. Place a slice of tuna on the other side of the plate and serve immediately.

CHEF'S NOTES:

The dressings all can be made a week in advance, covered, and refrigerated until ready to use.

VARIATIONS:

Instead of tuna you can use *hamachi* or salmon for this dish.

BEST SEASON:

Spring and summer are great times for this light dish; however, it can be made any time of the year.

GARAM MASALA VEGETABLE SALAD

The toasted-spice aroma of garam masala will linger in the air even after you prepare this vegetable salad, enticing everyone to ask, "What smells so good?" It's all about robust flavors inviting you to eat your vegetables.

EXPERIENCE LEVEL: ②
YIELD: 4–6 SERVINGS

VEGETABLES

3 portobello mushrooms, sliced

1 medium zucchini, diced

1 medium yellow squash, diced

1 small yellow onion, diced

4 large garlic cloves, smashed

3 teaspoons peeled and grated fresh ginger

2 teaspoons garam masala

½ cup vegetable oil

Salt and pepper to taste

Preheat the oven to 350°F.

Place the portobello slices in one bowl and the diced zucchini and squash in another bowl. Mix the remaining ingredients in a separate bowl and divide it between the mushrooms and squashes, tossing to coat. Keeping them separate, place the vegetables on two sheet trays and roast until tender, about 10–15 minutes.

GARAM MASALA AIOLI

1 cup mayonnaise

½ cup seeded and chopped plum tomato

⅓ cup finely chopped onion

1 teaspoon garam masala

¼ teaspoon salt

Combine all ingredients in a blender and puree until smooth. Set aside.

NAAN BREAD

1 teaspoon olive oil

Salt and pepper to taste

3 whole naan breads

Mix oil with salt and pepper. Brush on naan bread and lightly toast. Cut into bite-size triangles.

ASSEMBLY:

Lay out the portobellos on a plate, sprinkle with the zucchini and yellow squash, and drizzle aioli over vegetables, dotting any remaining aioli around the edge of the plate. Serve with naan triangles.

CHEF'S NOTES:

This dish can also be served cold or room temperature. The aioli can be made several days ahead and refrigerated up to a week.

VARIATIONS:

Using different flavored masalas will change the profile of this dish.

BEST SEASON:

This is a great light summer dish. It can also be used as a side dish for a brunch or dinner buffet.

BIG BITES
Entree Style

When you're planning a more formal dinner, you don't have to stick to the traditional main courses. One of the most impressive ways to wow your guests is to twist an old favorite into something unexpected.

Too often the home cook thinks in terms of meat, potato, and vegetable. That's certainly a great starting point, but now take it to the next level and think about adding layers to that dish. Instead of a steak and baked potato, try an oven-roasted veal loin with a roasted potato-mushroom stack. You love barbecue? Try slow roasting a pork shank and serve it with homemade onion rings and sautéed greens.

Think about what you love most in your favorite dishes, and then twist them up with something new and fresh. Take lasagna for instance. Instead of using ricotta cheese, try layering the pasta with cauliflower puree. Not only does it add richness to the dish, but it gets a serving of vegetables in there without anyone knowing!

Whether you're planning an intimate evening for two, a dinner party for ten, or a large family gathering, big bites are heartier dishes that move beyond a typical main course for an event of any size. They create a symphony of a meal with multiple flavors, textures, and presentations that are still simple to create but built to wow.

SCALLOPS AND SHRIMP WITH WATERMELON, AVOCADO, AND MINT SALSA

This light, refreshing recipe is great for a heavy hors d'oeuvres dinner party. Seared sea scallops and shrimp are paired with a salad of silky avocado and crisp watermelon and accented with mint and garlic. Can't you imagine the fragrance of summer?

EXPERIENCE LEVEL: ②
YIELD: 4 SERVINGS

WATERMELON, AVOCADO, AND MINT SALSA

2 cups seedless watermelon cubes

2 ripe -, peeled, seeded, and diced

1 tablespoon minced fresh cilantro

½ teaspoon chopped fresh mint

1 tablespoon chopped jalapeño pepper

½ cup chopped green bell peppers

2 tablespoons fresh-squeezed lime juice

1 tablespoon chopped scallions

½ tablespoon garlic salt

Combine all the ingredients in a medium bowl. Mix well. Serve immediately, or cover and refrigerate up to 1 hour.

MINT AND HORNED MELON SAUCE

1 horned melon

3 tablespoons fresh-squeezed lime juice

1 tablespoon prepared yellow mustard, plus more
    if necessary

1 teaspoon vegetable oil

¼ teaspoon ground cumin

1 garlic clove, minced

¼ teaspoon chopped fresh mint

Salt and pepper to taste

Cut the horned melon in half lengthwise and use a spoon to scoop out the pulp. Place the melon pulp, lime juice, mustard, oil, cumin, garlic, mint, salt, and pepper in a food processor and blend well.

Once the sauce is combined, give it a quick taste to make sure you like the flavors. You can add more salt and pepper to taste, or even more mustard if you want a thicker sauce.

SCALLOPS AND SHRIMP

12 large scallops

8 jumbo shrimp (approximately 10 per pound count)

3 teaspoons olive oil

Salt and pepper to taste

Brush both sides of the scallops or shrimp with olive oil, season with salt and pepper, and let sit for 10 minutes. In a heavy skillet, heat the remaining olive oil or add enough to lightly coat the bottom of the pan on medium-high until hot but not smoking. Pan sear the scallops for 1–2 minutes on each side; the sides on the scallops must be slightly browned. Cook the shrimp, searing until just pink and cooked through.

ASSEMBLY:

Spread 2 tablespoons of sauce along one side of each plate. Layer 3 scallops and 2 shrimp on top of the sauce. Portion the salad on the other side of the plate, and serve.

CHEF'S NOTES:

While this dish may seem a little complicated with a few moving parts, it is well worth the effort.

VARIATIONS:

You can substitute 6 kiwi fruit for the horned melon.

Instead of scallops and shrimp, try using lobster and tuna.

BEST SEASON:

This light dish is best for spring and summer. Serve with a light Chardonnay or an IPA.

OVEN-ROASTED DUCK BREAST WITH ROASTED FENNEL AND PEACH SALSA

I love the contrast of fresh-cut ripe fruit and caramelized, softened fennel. Peaches and fennel star in a salsa that is flavored with citrus and cilantro, creating the perfect accompaniment to roasted duck. The recipe can also be expanded for as many duck breasts as you need.

EXPERIENCE LEVEL: ②
YIELD: 4–6 SERVINGS

OVEN-ROASTED DUCK BREAST

4 Muscovy duck breasts

Salt and pepper to taste

2 tablespoons honey

3 tablespoons Alessi Ginger Infused White Balsamic Reduction

1 tablespoon fresh-squeezed lime juice

Score fat on duck breasts in a crisscross pattern in 1-inch intervals. Mix salt and pepper, honey, infused balsamic reduction, and lime juice together in a dish; brush the mixture over both sides of the duck breasts and place the breasts in a dish. Cover and allow to marinate at least 1 hour at room temperature or up to 24 hours in the refrigerator.

Preheat the oven to 175°F. Place a large, heavy skillet, preferably nonstick, over high heat. When the pan is hot, remove the duck breasts from the marinade; reserve it for a sauce, if desired. Place duck breasts in the skillet, skin side down, and sear for about 2 minutes, just until the skin is well browned. Remove the duck breasts from the skillet. Pour all the fat out of the skillet (reserve the fat for sauce or other cooking, if desired). Return the duck breasts to the skillet, skin side up, and cook for about 1 minute, just until the meat is seared. Transfer the duck breasts, skin side up, to a baking dish that will hold them in a single layer.

Place in the preheated oven for about an hour. By this time, the duck breasts will be uniformly pink throughout. They can remain in the oven as long as 2 hours and can stay warm even longer if the oven is turned off after 2 hours.

ROASTED FENNEL

4 tablespoons olive oil, plus more oil for the baking dish

4 fennel bulbs

Salt and freshly ground black pepper to taste

⅓ cup freshly shredded Parmesan, for assembly

Preheat the oven to 375°F. Lightly oil the bottom of a 13 x 9 x 2-inch glass baking dish. Shave fennel paper thin. Sprinkle with salt and pepper, drizzle with the oil, and toss. Reduce oven temperature to 300°F and bake until the fennel is fork tender and golden brown, about 15–20 minutes.

PEACH SALSA

4 small ripe peaches, peeled and diced

¼ cup orange juice

2 teaspoons Alessi Ginger Infused White Balsamic Reduction

2–3 tablespoons diced red bell pepper

1 tablespoon finely minced seeded jalapeño pepper, or to taste

1 heaping tablespoon chopped fresh cilantro

1 small clove garlic, finely minced

2 tablespoons finely chopped red onion

Combine all ingredients and refrigerate until serving time. The flavors are best if the salsa is refrigerated for 4 hours or overnight.

ASSEMBLY:

Slice the duck ¼ to ½ inch thick on an angle, and layer the duck slices on 4–6 plates sprinkled with a bit of Parmesan cheese. Combine fennel and peach salsa, portion onto each plate, and serve.

CHEF'S NOTES:

The duck in this dish can be grilled instead of pan seared and roasted.

VARIATIONS:

Make this dish with chicken or pork, or change the protein to tofu for a vegan dish.

BEST SEASON:

This dish is best in warm weather and early fall.

CHICKEN AND GARLIC-VEGETABLE FARRO

This dish is a great, nutritious blend of oven-roasted chicken and farro, a grain that is considered a superfood. Wholesome and delicious, farro and hearty vegetables deliver the flavor and healthy edge that we need to balance a meal.

EXPERIENCE LEVEL: ②
YIELD: 4–6 SERVINGS

ROASTED CHICKEN

1 (6-pound) roasting chicken
Salt and freshly ground black pepper to taste
2 medium onions, peeled and sliced crosswise
　½ inch thick
1 lemon
3 large cloves garlic, peeled
4 sprigs fresh thyme
2 tablespoons unsalted butter, softened
1 cup homemade chicken stock

Preheat the oven to 425°F. Remove and discard the plastic pop-up timer from the chicken, if there is one. Remove the giblets and excess fat from the chicken cavity. Rinse the chicken inside and out under cold running water and dry thoroughly with paper towels. Tuck the wing tips under the body. Sprinkle the cavity with salt and pepper, and set aside.

Place the onion slices in the center of a heavy-duty roasting pan. Pierce the entire surface of the lemon with a fork. Using the side of a large knife blade, gently press on the garlic cloves to open slightly. Insert garlic cloves, thyme sprigs, and lemon into the chicken cavity. Set the chicken in the roasting pan on the onion slices. Cut about 18 inches of kitchen twine, bring chicken legs forward, cross them, and tie them together. Spread the softened butter over the entire surface of the chicken, and sprinkle liberally with salt and pepper. Pour in the chicken stock. Place in the oven, and roast for 15 minutes, then drop temperature to 325°F and

roast until skin is deep golden brown and crisp and the juices run clear when pierced, about 1¼ hours. When chicken seems done, insert an instant-read thermometer into the breast, then the thigh. The breast temperature should read 155°F and the thigh 160°F. Remove chicken from oven, and transfer to a cutting board with a well (if possible). Let chicken stand 10–15 minutes so the juices settle.

GARLIC-VEGETABLE FARRO

2 tablespoons extra-virgin olive oil
1 each small onion, small carrot, and celery rib,
　all diced
1 medium zucchini, diced into ¼-inch pieces
1 medium yellow squash, diced into ¼-inch pieces
1 small rosemary sprig
4 scallions, thinly sliced, using the entire scallion
2 garlic cloves, minced
⅔ cup (4 ounces) farro, rinsed and drained
2 cups chicken stock or low-sodium broth
2 cups water
Pinch of salt
1 tablespoon unsalted butter
Freshly ground pepper to taste

In a large saucepan, heat 2 tablespoons oil. Add the onion, carrot, celery, zucchini, squash, rosemary, scallions, and garlic; cook over high heat, stirring, until just softened. Add the farro and cook, stirring, for 1 minute. Add the stock, water, and a pinch of salt; bring to a boil. Cover and cook over moderately high heat, stirring occasionally, until

the farro is tender, 15 minutes. Drain the farro, reserving ¼ cup cooking liquid for assembly, and taste, adding additional salt and pepper if needed.

ASSEMBLY:

Serve this dish family style as shown, using some of the reserved cooking liquid to moisten if needed.

CHEF'S NOTES:

Be sure to wash the farro before using. Sometimes during importation it becomes dusty.

VARIATIONS:

Use pork, veal, or lamb in place of chicken.

BEST SEASON:

This is a perfect fall-weather dish. It can be used as an enhancement to a brunch buffet for your friends and family.

SCALLOP MINESTRONE

I like the concept of a soup that has no strict recipe but consists of seasonal vegetables, beans, and some sort of pasta. I like playing with different combinations and noodle shapes, but this version, without pasta, is perfect to crown with pan-roasted sea scallops.

EXPERIENCE LEVEL: ②
YIELD: 4–6 SERVINGS

2 cups dried white lima or kidney beans

½ cup corn, fresh-cut from 2 cobs or frozen

½ cup peas, fresh or frozen

5 tablespoons extra-virgin olive oil, divided

2 cups diced carrots

2 cups diced yellow onions

1½ cups diced celery

5 garlic cloves, sliced

½ teaspoon dried thyme

1 bay leaf

2 tablespoons tomato paste

2 cups Gewürztraminer, Sauternes, or Riesling wine

8 cups vegetable stock

2 teaspoons salt

¼ teaspoon black pepper

1 pound sea scallops

1 cup finely julienned collard greens

2 teaspoons fresh lemon juice

¼ cup grated Parmigiano-Reggiano for garnish

1 tablespoon fresh thyme leaves for garnish

Cover beans with water and soak overnight.

Place a stockpot over medium heat. Combine 2 tablespoons olive oil, carrots, onions, and celery in the saucepan. Sweat until onions are translucent, 3–4 minutes. Add garlic, thyme, and bay leaf and cook for 1 minute. Add tomato paste, incorporating well. Deglaze pan with wine. Drain the beans and add them. Add stock and bring to a simmer. Reduce heat to low, cover, and simmer for 45–60 minutes, or until beans are tender. The soup may be prepared ahead of time to this point, and refrigerated if it is held more than briefly.

Season scallops with salt and pepper. In a sauté pan over medium heat, add 2 tablespoons olive oil, then sear scallops. Shortly before serving, reheat the soup. Add scallops, collard greens, lemon juice, salt, and pepper. Simmer another 2 minutes, or until scallops are cooked. Divide soup among warmed bowls. Sprinkle with cheese, thyme, and remaining tablespoon of olive oil.

CHEF'S NOTES:

This dish can be a great main course, or in smaller portions as a starter.

VARIATIONS:

Use shrimp in place of scallops or finish with jumbo lump crabmeat.

BEST SEASON:

This is a great fall or late-summer dish. Served with a light Chardonnay or Pinot Grigio.

OVEN-ROASTED PORK LOIN WITH PICKLED RED ONIONS AND BRAISED CHERRIES

Pork loves braised fruit, and cherries really accentuate the roasted flavor of the loin. Pickling the onions reduces their "bite" and replaces it with acidity, sweetness, and spice.

EXPERIENCE LEVEL: ③
YIELD: 4–6 SERVINGS

OVEN-ROASTED PORK LOIN

3 cloves garlic, peeled and minced

1 tablespoon dried rosemary

Salt and pepper to taste

2 pounds boneless pork loin roast

¼ cup olive oil

½ cup white wine

Preheat the oven to 350°F.

Crush garlic with rosemary, salt, and pepper, making a paste. Pierce the meat with a sharp knife in several places and press the garlic paste into the openings. Place the meat in a small roasting pan, rub it with the remaining garlic mixture, and pour the olive oil over it. Place pork loin in preheated oven, turning and basting occasionally with pan liquids. Cook about 1 hour, until the pork is no longer pink in the center and an instant-read thermometer inserted into the center reads 155°F. Remove roast to a platter. Deglaze the pan with the wine, stirring to loosen the browned bits on the bottom, and reserve liquid for braising cherries.

PICKLED RED ONIONS

¾ cup Alessi White Balsamic Pear Infused Vinegar (or any quality Champagne vinegar)

¼ cup orange juice

3 teaspoons fresh-squeezed lime juice

1 pint red pearl onions, peeled

1 tablespoon sugar

1 tablespoon salt

2 bay leaves

1 teaspoon coriander seeds

Combine all ingredients and place in a saucepan. Heat to 125°F over medium heat. Once the temperature is reached, remove from the heat, and allow the mixture to steep until the onions are soft, about 45 minutes.

BRAISED CHERRIES

3 tablespoons unsalted butter, divided

2 leeks, including pale green parts, halved, well washed, and thinly sliced

½ cup chicken broth

½ cup liquid from deglazing of pork

¼ cup port wine

2 tablespoons Alessi Premium Balsamic Reduction (or any quality balsamic reduction)

½ cup dried cherries

Melt 2 tablespoons butter in a saucepan over medium heat. Add the leeks and sauté until softened and beginning to brown, 3–4 minutes. Stir in the broth and cook, stirring to scrape up any browned bits on the pan bottom, for 1 minute. Stir in the wine, vinegar reduction, cherries, and remaining tablespoon butter.

BUTTERNUT SQUASH HASH

6–7 bacon strips, chopped
½ medium yellow onion
1 medium butternut squash, peeled and seeded
2 small red potatoes
1 cup chicken stock
4 fresh sage leaves, chopped
Salt and pepper to taste

Set a large sauté pan over medium-low heat. Add chopped bacon. Cook slowly until crispy, allowing the fat to render, then remove the crisp bacon and reserve.

While the bacon cooks, prepare vegetables by chopping the onions and cutting the squash and potatoes into a medium dice. Add the onion to the pan with the bacon fat and cook until softened. Add the squash, potatoes, and stock, and increase the heat to medium-high. Cook, stirring occasionally, until squash and potatoes are cooked and the stock is evaporated. Add sage, salt, and pepper. Cook another minute or two and stir in the bacon.

RED WINE DEMI-GLACE

4 tablespoons cold unsalted butter
3 tablespoons diced shallots
2 teaspoons dried tarragon
1 cup dry red wine
1¼ cups demi-glace
1 teaspoon salt, plus more as needed
1 teaspoon Dijon mustard

Melt 2 tablespoons butter in a sauté pan. Add the diced shallots and sauté over low heat until they are soft and clear. Add the tarragon and red wine. Increase heat to medium and reduce the wine by 75 percent. Add the prepared demi-glace and simmer. Whisk in the salt and Dijon mustard. Turn off the heat and adjust the salt. Cut the remaining butter into pieces and whip it in quickly, one piece at a time, to fully incorporate the butter into the sauce.

ASSEMBLY:

Slice pork loin into ¼-inch slices, lay on plates, and top with braised cherries and pickled onions. Spoon the butternut squash hash on one side. Drizzle red wine demi-glace onto pork slices and serve.

CHEF'S NOTES:

The onions and the hash can be made a day ahead of time and reheated.

VARIATIONS:

As an option, change the pork to veal, use mushrooms instead of butternut squash, and switch the cherry sauce to blueberry sauce.

BEST SEASON:

This is a great holiday dinner dish for the winter months.

PAN-ROASTED SNAPPER WITH MANILA CLAMS AND SWEET POTATO RAGOUT

Snapper is a slightly sweet, mild, and firm fish. It benefits from this bite's briny and spicy yet sweet sauce created by the mélange of manila clams, poblano peppers, and sweet potato.

EXPERIENCE LEVEL: ②
YIELD: 4 SERVINGS

CLAMS AND SWEET-POTATO RAGOUT

3 poblano peppers

1 tablespoon olive oil

½ onion, peeled and diced

1 carrot, peeled and diced

2 ribs celery, diced

2 ears corn, kernels removed and cobs reserved

1 large sweet potato, peeled and diced

1 bay leaf

⅛ teaspoon cayenne

⅛ teaspoon smoked paprika

⅛ teaspoon fresh thyme, chopped

Pinch of cinnamon

Salt and pepper to taste

6 ounces unsweetened coconut milk

2 dozen manila clams

Preheat the broiler. Put poblano peppers under the hot broiler, rotating and cooking them on all sides until they are charred. Place blackened peppers in a plastic bag, seal, and allow them to steam for 10 minutes. Remove peppers from the bag and peel off the translucent top layer of skin. Seed and dice.

Heat the oil in an 8-quart saucepan over medium heat. Add the onion, carrot, and celery and cook until tender. Add the corn and corn cobs, sweet potato, diced poblano peppers, bay leaf, cayenne, smoked paprika, thyme, cinnamon, salt, and pepper. Add water to cover the ingredients. Bring to a boil and simmer for about 20 minutes. Remove the corn cobs. Add coconut milk and bring to a boil. Cook for

an additional 5 minutes. Add clams, cooking until they all open, discarding any that do not.

PAN-ROASTED SNAPPER

4 (4–5-ounce) fillets red snapper

1 tablespoon olive oil

Juice of 1 lemon

2 tablespoons rice wine vinegar

1 teaspoon Dijon mustard

1 tablespoon honey

¼ cup chopped scallions

1 teaspoon peeled and grated fresh ginger

Rinse snapper under cold water and pat dry. In a shallow bowl, mix together the remaining ingredients. Heat a nonstick skillet over medium heat. Dip each snapper fillet in marinade to coat both sides, cover, and refrigerate for 10 minutes. Place fish in skillet and cook for 2–3 minutes on each side and set aside. Pour remaining marinade into skillet. Reduce heat, and simmer 2–3 minutes to reduce slightly. Reserve for assembly.

ASSEMBLY:

Cut the snapper fillets in half. Spoon reduction equally onto four dinner plates, then place a half fillet on top, off center. Spoon 1 tablespoon of ragout onto each snapper half. Cover ragout with another half fillet. Toss remaining ragout with clams, divide evenly among the plates, and serve.

CHEF'S NOTES:

This quick dish requires only two pans: one to sear the fish and another to cook the ragout.

VARIATIONS:

Instead of snapper, use tilefish or sea bass; substitute mussels for the clams.

BEST SEASON:

This is a great fall dish.

OVEN-ROASTED VEAL LOIN WITH ROASTED POTATO–MUSHROOM STACK

I often envision the shape my dishes will take before I even consider flavors or components. I call this "boxing," and it gives me the foundation to build on. Think about the plates you're using, the theme of the evening, the personalities of your guests, and "box" them all into the perfect meal!

EXPERIENCE LEVEL: ②
YIELD: 4 SERVINGS

ROASTED VEAL LOIN

2 pounds boned veal loin

Salt and pepper to taste

⅓ cup Dijon mustard

8 bacon slices, or enough to cover the roast

1 garlic head, separated into cloves and peeled

12 shallots, peeled

½ cup dry white wine

3 teaspoons finely chopped fresh tarragon, divided, plus tarragon sprigs for garnish

Preheat the oven to 325°F.

Season the veal with salt and pepper, spread the mustard over the top and sides, and cover the veal with the bacon. Arrange the veal, garlic, and shallots in a roasting pan just large enough to hold them. Add the wine and roast the veal in the middle of the oven, basting every 5 minutes, for 40 minutes or until an instant-read thermometer registers 150°F. Transfer the veal to a cutting board and let it stand, covered loosely with foil, for 15 minutes. Transfer the garlic and the shallots with a slotted spoon to a bowl, toss them with 2 teaspoons chopped tarragon, and keep them warm, covered with foil.

While the veal is standing, skim the fat from the pan juices, add ¼ cup water, and deglaze the pan over high heat, scraping up the brown bits, until the mixture is reduced by half. Strain the mixture through a fine sieve into a bowl, and season this gravy with salt and pepper.

POTATO CRISPS

¼ cup olive oil

2 large baking potatoes, peeled and thinly sliced

Salt and pepper to taste

Preheat the oven to 375°F.

Brush two large baking sheets generously with oil. Arrange the potato slices on them in one layer. Brush the potatoes with the remaining oil and top with another two baking sheets to keep the potatoes from curling. Bake till golden brown, about 30–35 minutes. Transfer to cooling racks and season with salt and pepper.

MUSHROOM FILLING

½ cup sliced shallots

3 tablespoons unsalted butter

12 ounces assorted fresh mushrooms, cleaned and sliced

1 teaspoon salt

½ teaspoon freshly ground black pepper

1 cup chicken stock

1 cup heavy cream

2 teaspoons chopped fresh thyme

2 tablespoons white truffle oil

¾ cup grated Asiago cheese, for serving

In a skillet over medium heat, cook the shallots in butter for about 1 minute. Add the mushrooms, salt, and pepper and cook until soft and most of the mushroom liquid has evaporated, about 8 minutes.

Add the stock, cream, and thyme and simmer for about 5 minutes or until the liquid has reduced by half. Remove from the heat and add the truffle oil.

ROASTED PEPPER SAUCE

1 (12-ounce) jar roasted red peppers, drained
⅓ cup vegetable broth
1 large clove garlic, chopped
3 tablespoons chopped fresh chives
3 tablespoons chopped fresh basil
1 tablespoon Alessi Balsamic Vinegar (or other quality balsamic vinegar)

Combine all ingredients in a blender or food processor and blend until smooth.

ASSEMBLY:

Place two crispy potato slices on each of four plates. Spoon a generous spoonful of the mushroom mixture onto the potato slices. Sprinkle with some of the grated Asiago cheese. Repeat until you have three layers, ending with the mushrooms on top. Nestle the veal loin alongside and drizzle the roasted pepper sauce around the meat and the potato stacks.

CHEF'S NOTES:

The potatoes can be made up to five days ahead of time and reheated on the day of use.

VARIATIONS:

Substitute pork loin, lamb, or chicken for the veal.

BEST SEASON:

Fall or winter.

SEARED SALMON WITH WARM FENNEL COUSCOUS AND GARLIC LEMON SAUCE

I love this dish in late summer. The flavors are simple and clean. If you buy the freshest fish, all it needs is olive oil and lemon. This anise-scented couscous complements the salmon.

EXPERIENCE LEVEL: ②
YIELD: 4 SERVINGS

WARM FENNEL COUSCOUS

1 cup uncooked Israeli couscous

1½ cups vegetable stock

1 small bulb fennel, shaved thin

1 small shallot, thinly sliced

1 tablespoon fresh-squeezed lemon juice

1 tablespoon plus 1 teaspoon olive oil

½ teaspoon salt

¼ teaspoon freshly ground black pepper

Cook couscous in vegetable stock according to the package instructions, until all the stock is absorbed and couscous is tender but not mushy. In a large bowl, combine the cooked couscous, fennel, shallot, lemon juice, 1 tablespoon oil, salt, and pepper.

At serving time, heat the remaining teaspoon of oil in a large nonstick skillet over medium-high heat. Add fennel-couscous mix and lightly sauté just to warm, about 3–5 minutes.

SALMON

4 (6-ounce) center-cut salmon fillets

1½ tablespoons fresh-squeezed lemon juice

1½ tablespoons olive oil

Salt and freshly ground black pepper to taste

Place the salmon fillets in a shallow bowl. Cover with lemon juice, olive oil, salt, and pepper. Let rest for 15 minutes.

Cook the salmon, skin side down, in a nonstick skillet over medium-high heat for 2–3 minutes, shaking the pan and carefully lifting the salmon with a spatula to loosen it from the pan and turn over.

Reduce the heat to medium and cook until salmon is cooked through, 3–4 minutes more. The skin should be crisp and the flesh medium rare.

GARLIC-LEMON SAUCE

½ cup unsalted butter

2 tablespoons fresh-squeezed lemon juice

2 cloves garlic, sliced

Salt and pepper to taste

Heat half the butter in a sauté pan over medium heat. Add garlic and lightly brown. Add lemon juice and allow to reduce slightly. Finish with remaining butter and season to taste.

ASSEMBLY:

Place 2 tablespoons couscous salad in the middle of each plate. Split each seared salmon fillet in half and stack it on top. Drizzle garlic-lemon sauce on top and around the salmon.

CHEF'S NOTES:

Buy your fish from a knowledgeable source and look for fresh salmon fillet.

VARIATIONS:

You can use cod, swordfish, shrimp, scallops, or chicken as a variation.

BEST SEASON:

This is great for a late-summer dish; serve with a Chardonnay, Pinot Grigio, or a light pale ale.

OVEN-ROASTED PORK LOIN, MUSHROOM RAGOUT, AND TOMATO-STEAMED CLAMS

Everybody loves these flavors—tomatoes and clams steamed with oregano and thyme, roast pork accented with garlic and rosemary, and wild mushrooms in a rich creamy demi-glace.

EXPERIENCE LEVEL: ②
YIELD: 4–6 SERVINGS

OVEN-ROASTED PORK LOIN

4 large garlic cloves, pressed
4 teaspoons chopped fresh rosemary
   (or 2 teaspoons dried)
1½ teaspoons coarse salt
½ teaspoon freshly ground black pepper
2½ pounds boneless pork loin roast, well trimmed

Preheat the oven to 400°F.

Line a 13 × 9 × 2-inch roasting pan with foil. Mix first four ingredients in bowl; rub mixture all over the pork. Place pork, fat side down, in prepared roasting pan. Roast 30 minutes, then turn the pork fat side up. Roast until thermometer inserted into center registers 155°F, about 25 minutes longer. Remove from oven; let stand 10 minutes.

WILD MUSHROOM RAGOUT

1 pound mixed fresh wild mushrooms, such as
   black trumpets, fairy rings, and cèpes
1 tablespoon unsalted butter or olive oil
2 shallots, peeled and finely chopped
1 clove garlic, peeled and minced
¾ cup chicken stock
3 tablespoons demi-glace or reduced veal
   stock, optional
¼ cup heavy cream
2 sprigs fresh thyme
1 tablespoon chopped fresh chives
Salt and freshly ground black pepper to taste

Trim the mushrooms, reserving stems for another use. Slice large caps into fairly even pieces; leave smaller caps intact. Melt butter (or heat oil) in a large skillet over medium heat. Add shallots and garlic, and cook until tender, stirring occasionally, about 15 minutes. Add mushroom caps and cook until they release their liquid. Add chicken stock and cook for about 5 more minutes. Stir in demi-glace, if using, and cream, and cook for another 5 minutes. Add thyme and chives, then season to taste with salt and pepper.

TOMATO-STEAMED CLAMS

1 teaspoon olive oil
½ cup chopped onion
1 teaspoon chopped fresh oregano
1 teaspoon chopped fresh rosemary
1 teaspoon chopped fresh thyme
1½ cups dry white wine
½ cup fat-free, low-sodium chicken broth
¼ teaspoon freshly ground black pepper
1 (14.5-ounce) can diced tomatoes, undrained
48 manila clams in shells, scrubbed (about 3 pounds)
1 tablespoon chopped fresh parsley

Heat a Dutch oven over medium-high heat, add oil, and swirl to coat. Add onion, oregano, rosemary, and thyme; sauté 2 minutes. Add white wine, broth, pepper, and tomatoes and bring to a boil. Stir in clams; cover and cook 5 minutes or until clams open. Discard any unopened shells. Keep warm.

ASSEMBLY:

Slice pork loin into ¼-inch pieces and divide it among the plates. Spoon all of wild mushroom ragout onto or alongside the pork, dividing evenly. Distribute steamed clams on the plates next to the pork.

CHEF'S NOTES:

The components can be served together or as separate dishes. I suggest College Inn Bold if you need to use canned chicken broth.

VARIATIONS:

Use veal, lamb, or even chicken for this dish.

BEST SEASON:

This is a great fall dish.

BARBECUE BRAISED PORK SHANKS

The shank is a tough cut of meat until you braise it low and slow, tenderizing the meat until it literally starts to melt off the bone. It will warm the kitchen while it's cooking, so this is a great dish to make when it's frigid outside. I like to slather it in barbecue sauce, making it reminiscent of a summer cookout.

EXPERIENCE LEVEL: ②
YIELD: 6 SERVINGS

BARBECUE BRAISED PORK SHANKS

½ cup all-purpose flour

2 tablespoons chili powder

1 tablespoon salt, plus more as needed

1 tablespoon freshly ground black pepper,
    plus more as needed

6 (1½-pound) pork shanks

¼ cup extra-virgin olive oil

1 medium onion, peeled and chopped

2 medium carrots, peeled and chopped

2 medium celery ribs, chopped

6 garlic cloves, peeled and minced

1 cup dry white wine

6 cups chicken stock or low-sodium broth

3 rosemary sprigs

2 bay leaves

2 thyme sprigs

In a large, sturdy, resealable plastic bag, combine the flour and chili powder with 1 tablespoon each of salt and pepper. Add the pork shanks, one at a time, and shake to coat thoroughly.

In a large skillet, heat 2 tablespoons olive oil until shimmering. Add three of the pork shanks and cook over moderately high heat until browned all over, about 10 minutes. Transfer the browned shanks to a deep, heavy casserole. Wipe out the skillet and brown the remaining three pork shanks in the remaining 2 tablespoons olive oil; lower the heat if necessary to keep them from browning too much. Add to the casserole. Add the onion, carrots, celery, and garlic to the skillet and cook over moderate heat until softened, about 5 minutes. Add the wine and bring to a boil. Simmer until slightly reduced, about 2 minutes. Pour the wine and vegetables over the pork. Add the stock, rosemary, bay leaves, and thyme, season with salt and pepper, and bring to a boil. Tuck the pork shanks into the liquid so that they're mostly submerged. Cover and cook over moderately low heat for 2½ hours, or until the meat is very tender. Turn the pork shanks every 30 minutes to keep them submerged in the liquid.

Transfer the braised shanks to a large, deep platter; cover and keep warm. Strain the liquid, pressing hard on the solids; discard the solids. Return the liquid to the casserole and boil until reduced to 4 cups, about 20 minutes. Spoon off the fat and keep warm.

ROASTED SLICED POTATOES

1¼ pounds Idaho potatoes, sliced ⅛ inch thick

2 tablespoons olive oil

¾ teaspoon salt

¼ teaspoon freshly ground black pepper

Preheat the oven to 425°F and place a rimmed baking sheet on the center rack. Toss the potatoes with the oil, salt, and pepper. Carefully spread the slices on the hot baking sheet in a single layer and roast until golden and crispy, 30–35 minutes, turning with a metal spatula occasionally and spreading them out to cook evenly.

FRIED ONION RINGS

1 quart vegetable oil for frying

1 cup all-purpose flour

1 cup beer

Pinch of salt

Pinch of freshly ground black pepper

4 onions, peeled and sliced into rings ½ inch thick

In a large, deep skillet, heat oil to 365°F. In a medium bowl, combine flour, beer, salt, and pepper. Mix until smooth. Dredge and evenly coat the onion slices in the batter. Deep-fry the onions in the hot oil until golden brown, approximately 3–6 minutes. Drain on paper towels.

SAUTÉED GARLIC SPINACH

1½ pounds baby spinach leaves

2 tablespoons good-quality olive oil

2 tablespoons chopped garlic (about 6 cloves)

2 teaspoons salt

¾ teaspoon freshly ground black pepper

1 tablespoon unsalted butter

Lemon

Sea salt (optional)

Rinse the spinach well in cold water to make sure it's very clean. Spin it dry in a salad spinner, leaving just a little water clinging to the leaves. In a very large pot or Dutch oven, heat the olive oil and sauté the garlic over medium heat for about 1 minute; do not brown. Add the spinach, salt, and pepper to the pot, toss it with the garlic and oil, cover the pot, and cook for 2 minutes. Uncover the pot, turn the heat to high, and cook the spinach for another minute, stirring with a wooden spoon, until all the spinach is wilted. Using a slotted spoon, lift the spinach to a serving bowl and top with the butter, a squeeze of lemon, and a sprinkling of sea salt if desired. Serve hot.

ASSEMBLY:

Place sliced potatoes on one side of each plate and top with a pork shank. Drizzle 2 tablespoons braising liquid over each pork shank. On the other side of the plate, stack 3 or 4 onion rings, creating a cylinder, fill with spinach, and serve.

CHEF'S NOTES:

To intensify its flavor, the pork shank can be made two days ahead. If prepared in advance, reheat to 145°F and continue with assembly.

VARIATIONS:

You can use lamb or beef shanks as a substitute. Depending on size, the cooking time may be different.

BEST SEASON:

Best served in fall and winter, but good year-round.

FRISÉE, APPLE, HONEY-CHILE ALMONDS, AND BACON CIDER DRESSING

I love the juxtaposition of sweet honey and spicy chile. That sweet heat continues to build on your palate as you devour this crunchy, smoky salad. Grilling the apples is a fun twist.

EXPERIENCE LEVEL: ②
YIELD: 4–6 SERVINGS

GRILLED APPLES

⅔ cup fresh orange juice

1 tablespoon chopped fresh mint

2 tablespoons honey

1 teaspoon vanilla extract

½ teaspoon ground ginger

¼ teaspoon freshly ground black pepper

3 Granny Smith apples, cored, each cut crosswise into 4 (½-inch) slices

Combine all the ingredients in a large ziplock plastic bag, seal, and marinate in refrigerator for 1–2 hours, turning bag occasionally.

Prepare the grill. Remove apple slices from the bag, reserving marinade. Place slices on grill rack coated with cooking spray; grill for about 6 minutes, turning and basting frequently with reserved marinade.

HONEY-CHILE ALMONDS

2 tablespoons sugar

¾ teaspoon salt

¼ cup honey

¾ teaspoon cayenne pepper

1–1½ cups sliced raw almonds

Preheat oven to 325°F. Line a rimmed baking sheet with parchment or waxed paper. If using parchment, lightly oil it. Combine the sugar and salt in a bowl large enough to accommodate the almonds and set aside.

Melt the honey in a large skillet over low to medium heat. Add the cayenne and the almonds and stir until all the nuts are coated with the honey and spice. Spread the nuts in a single layer on the baking sheet and bake for about 10 minutes. Let the almonds cool slightly and toss them in the sugar-salt mixture. Remove the parchment or waxed paper from the baking sheet and spread the almonds on it again to let them cool completely.

BACON CIDER DRESSING

½ cup prepared mustard

1 medium Granny Smith apple, unpeeled but cored and roughly chopped

½ cup cider vinegar

½ cup Alessi White Balsamic Pear Infused Vinegar (or any quality Champagne vinegar)

½ cup vegetable stock

6 tablespoons honey

1 cup olive oil

1¼ pounds bacon (about 20 slices), cooked and chopped

Combine all ingredients but oil and bacon in a blender and puree until smooth. Slowly incorporate oil, drizzling in a little at a time until smooth. Stir in the chopped bacon.

SALAD

3 heads frisée greens, cleaned and torn into bite-size pieces

ASSEMBLY:

Toss greens with vinaigrette to taste, and top with almonds and grilled apples.

CHEF'S NOTES:

Both the dressing and the almonds can be made a day ahead. Keep the almonds in an airtight container, and refrigerate the dressing.

VARIATIONS:

You can substitute Bibb lettuce or romaine, as long as the leaf is thick and can handle the weight of the dressing.

BEST SEASON:

This is a great salad for early spring or late summer as the weather begins to cool.

COD AND SHRIMP CAKES WITH CORN SALSA AND SUN-DRIED TOMATO TAPENADE

People who reside along the mid-Atlantic coast take pride in their local sweet corn and fresh seafood, and this recipe celebrates the bounty of the Atlantic Ocean and farm-stand fresh corn. In addition, these cod and shrimp cakes offer a more complex texture than a typical crab cake.

EXPERIENCE LEVEL: ②
YIELD: 4 SERVINGS

CORN SALSA

2 cups fresh corn kernels

¼ red onion, diced

1 jalapeño pepper, seeded and minced

½ bunch fresh cilantro, chopped

½ tomato, diced

Salt to taste

Pinch of chili powder

1 lime, plus more if desired

Mix the corn with the onion, jalapeño, cilantro, and tomato. Add a pinch of salt, a pinch of chili powder, and the juice of 1 lime. Taste and add more lime and salt as desired.

SUN-DRIED TOMATO TAPENADE

2 cups boiling water

1 cup sun-dried tomatoes

½ cup kalamata olives, pitted

2 tablespoons dried basil

2 tablespoons fresh lemon juice

1 garlic clove, minced

2 teaspoons olive oil

Combine boiling water and sun-dried tomatoes; cover and let stand 15 minutes or until soft. Drain tomatoes in a colander over a bowl, reserving ¾ cup liquid. Combine tomatoes, reserved liquid, olives, basil, lemon juice, and garlic in a blender or food processor; process until smooth. Place tomato mixture in a small bowl; stir in oil. Cover and chill.

COD AND SHRIMP CAKES

2 tablespoons finely diced carrot

¼ cup finely chopped onion

½ cup finely chopped fresh shiitake caps (about 2 large)

¼ cup dashi

¼ pound shrimp without heads, peeled, deveined, and finely chopped by hand or pulsed in a food processor

¼ pound cod fillet, finely chopped by hand or pulsed in a food processor

1 large egg yolk, lightly beaten

½ teaspoon fine sea salt

1 teaspoon light shoyu (Japanese soy sauce)

2 teaspoons sugar

1 cup canola oil for frying

Cook carrot, onion, and mushrooms in dashi, uncovered, in a small heavy skillet over moderate heat. Stir frequently until carrot and onion are softened, about 4 minutes. Cool slightly.

Stir together shrimp, fish, vegetable mixture, egg yolk, sea salt, shoyu, and sugar in a bowl until combined well, then knead with your hands to form a paste. Chill, covered, until cold, about 1 hour.

Heat oil in a deep 10-inch skillet over moderate heat until it registers 250°F on a thermometer. While oil is heating, form the shrimp-cod mixture into four ½-inch-thick cakes. Fry the cakes until light golden, about 2 minutes on each side, then transfer with a wide metal spatula to paper towels to drain. Flip over and drain again on a clean paper towel.

ASSEMBLY:

Divide corn salsa evenly among four plates. Top with a cod-shrimp cake. Spoon tapenade onto the side of the plate as a dipping sauce.

CHEF'S NOTES:

I really enjoy this dish. Its flavors, colors, and lightness on the palate make this fun for lunch or a brunch buffet.

VARIATIONS:

Use salmon instead of cod and scallops or monkfish in place of shrimp.

BEST SEASON:

This dish can be prepared in late spring and summer. It's light and goes great with a nice Chardonnay, Pinot Noir, or IPA.

BIBB LETTUCE WITH POMEGRANATE, ORANGE, TOASTED SUNFLOWER SEEDS, AND HERB VINAIGRETTE

The jewel-toned colors of ruby red, citrine orange, and emerald green just pop off the plate when this salad is composed. Yes, it's beautiful, but wait until you taste it!

EXPERIENCE LEVEL: ①
YIELD: 4–6 SERVINGS

HERB VINAIGRETTE

⅓ cup olive oil or salad oil

⅓ cup Alessi white or red wine vinegar, rice vinegar, or white vinegar

1–2 teaspoons sugar

1 tablespoon snipped fresh thyme, oregano, or basil, or ½ teaspoon dried thyme, oregano, or basil, crushed

¼ teaspoon dry mustard or 1 teaspoon Dijon mustard

1 clove garlic, minced

⅛ teaspoon freshly ground black pepper

In a blender combine all ingredients and mix until smooth.

SALAD

1 pomegranate

1 teaspoon balsamic vinegar

1 teaspoon Alessi Orange Blossom Honey Balsamic Vinegar

2 teaspoons extra-virgin olive oil

½ teaspoon salt

⅛ teaspoon freshly ground black pepper

2 heads Bibb lettuce, separated, washed, and dried

2 ripe oranges, peeled and segmented

½ cup shelled pepitas (pumpkin seeds), toasted

Cut the pomegranate in half. Remove seeds from one half, being careful not to burst the individual juice sacs; set seeds aside for garnish. Squeeze 2 tablespoons juice from other pomegranate half, using a citrus reamer or juicer. In a large bowl, combine pomegranate juice, both vinegars, oil, salt, and pepper, mixing vigorously with a whisk. Add lettuce; toss gently to coat. Divide lettuce among serving plates. Sprinkle orange segments, toasted pepitas, and pomegranate seeds on top. Serve immediately.

CHEF'S NOTES:

The dressing and the accompaniments can be prepared ahead of time and put together with the lettuce just before serving.

VARIATIONS:

You can change the lettuce to romaine hearts, oranges to apples, and the dressing to mustard vinaigrette.

BEST SEASON:

Great fall dish with a glass of Chardonnay or light IPA.

BUTTERNUT SQUASH RAVIOLI

This butternut squash–filled pasta is a hearty plate for fall, adored by meat eaters and vegetarians alike. The flavor of squash marries well with earthy mushrooms and sage.

EXPERIENCE LEVEL: ③
YIELD: 4–6 SERVINGS

RAVIOLI

1 tablespoon unsalted butter
3 tablespoons minced shallots
1 cup roasted butternut squash puree
Salt and freshly ground pepper to taste
3 tablespoons heavy cream
3 tablespoons grated Parmigiano-Reggiano cheese
Pinch of nutmeg
1 tablespoon finely chopped fresh sage
8 (6 x 6-inch) fresh or frozen pasta sheets
1 egg
1 teaspoon water

In a large sauté pan over medium heat, melt butter. Add the shallots and sauté for 1 minute. Add the squash puree and cook until the mixture is slightly dry, 2–3 minutes. Season with salt and pepper. Stir in the cream and continue to cook for 2 minutes. Remove from the heat and stir in cheese, nutmeg, and chopped sage. Let cool completely.

Cut each pasta sheet into 3-inch squares. Whisk egg and water together to form an egg wash. Place 2 teaspoons filling in the center of each pasta square. Brush egg wash on all 4 edges. Bring one corner of the square to the opposite corner, forming a triangle, and seal the pasta completely.

Add the pasta to a pot of boiling, salted water. Cook until al dente, 2–3 minutes, or until the pasta floats and is pale in color. Remove the pasta from the water and drain well.

TOPPING

½ cup unsalted butter
½ bunch fresh sage, leaves chopped, reserving 12 leaves for garnish
1 cup cremini mushrooms, stems removed and caps sliced
1 cup finely diced butternut squash
2 ounces Parmigiano-Reggiano cheese, grated

In a large sauté pan, melt the butter. Add the sage, mushrooms, and squash and continue to cook on low heat until squash is tender, about 10 minutes. Remove from the heat. Place some of the cooked ravioli in the center of each plate and spoon the sauce over it. Divide and sprinkle cheese evenly over each plate and garnish with sage leaves.

CHEF'S NOTES:

This hands-on recipe is fun to experiment with and easily created. Be patient with the process, and you will make a dish of beauty.

VARIATIONS:

The ravioli can be made with mushrooms chopped and tossed with garlic and rosemary in place of butternut squash.

BEST SEASON:

A great fall dish that goes perfectly with a Pinot Noir or a stout ale.

PAD THAI NOODLE

Here's traditional pad thai with an American twist: I top it with bacon!

EXPERIENCE LEVEL: ②
YIELD: 4–6 SERVINGS

PAD THAI SAUCE

⅓ cup flavorful chicken stock

3 tablespoons rice vinegar

1 tablespoon fresh-squeezed lime juice

3–4 tablespoons brown sugar

2 tablespoons fish sauce

1 tablespoon soy sauce

¼ teaspoon cayenne pepper

⅛ teaspoon pepper

Combine all sauce ingredients in a cup, stirring to dissolve the sugar. Set aside.

PAD THAI

1 boneless chicken breast, or 1 or 2 thighs, chopped small

1½ tablespoons soy sauce

9 ounces dried pad thai rice noodles

2–3 tablespoons vegetable oil for stir-frying

3–4 cloves garlic, minced

1 teaspoon peeled and grated fresh ginger

1–2 fresh red or green chiles, to taste, finely sliced

4 scallions, sliced (separate white from green parts)

1 egg

2–3 cups bean sprouts

⅓ cup chopped unsalted dry-roasted peanuts

8 bacon slices, cooked and chopped

Lime wedges for serving

Place chopped chicken in a bowl and toss with soy sauce. Set aside.

Bring a large pot of water to boil. Dunk in the rice noodles and remove the pot from the heat. Allow noodles to soak approximately 6 minutes, or until soft enough to bend easily, though still firm and undercooked by regular standards (this is key to good pad thai; the noodles will finish cooking when you stir-fry them later). Drain and rinse the noodles briefly with cold water to keep from sticking. Set aside.

Heat a wok or large frying pan over medium-high heat. Drizzle in the oil and swirl it around, then add the garlic, chiles, ginger, and the white parts of the scallions (reserve green tops for later). Stir-fry for 1 minute. Add marinated chicken and stir-fry until chicken is opaque, 2–3 minutes. When pan becomes dry, add 1–2 tablespoons of the pad thai sauce—just enough to keep ingredients cooking nicely. Using your spatula or cooking utensil, push ingredients to the side of the pan (if pan is dry, drizzle in a little oil). Crack egg into center and stir-fry quickly to scramble. Then add noodles plus 3–4 tablespoons of the pad thai sauce. Using two utensils, lift and turn the noodles to stir-fry them with other ingredients. Continue in this way, adding more sauce every minute or two, until all the sauce has been added and the noodles are chewy and a little sticky, 8–10 minutes. Take 1 more minute to gently fold in the bean sprouts (they will soften in the heat of the noodles while remaining crispy). Serve the pad thai garnished with green scallion tops, peanuts, bacon, and lime wedges.

CHEF'S NOTES:

This dish is nice and light and can be used as a side dish to complete a meal or as an entree.

VARIATIONS:

Add shrimp or pork to change this dish; instead of egg, use tofu to create a new protein combination.

BEST SEASON:

This dish can be used year-round and is a great healthier, lighter alternative to traditional pastas.

WILD MUSHROOM–STUFFED CHICKEN

This could be an elegant entree for a dinner party. The pan sauce is finished with Madeira, which I think always makes a sauce special and is a natural match with mushrooms.

EXPERIENCE LEVEL: ②
YIELD: 4 SERVINGS

WILD MUSHROOM STUFFING

1 teaspoon olive oil
12 ounces assorted wild mushrooms, stems trimmed, roughly chopped
½ teaspoon salt
¼ teaspoon freshly ground black pepper
2 tablespoons minced shallots
2 teaspoons minced garlic
2 tablespoons dry white wine
2 tablespoons freshly grated Parmesan
1 cup fine dried bread crumbs
2 teaspoons chopped fresh parsley
1½ teaspoons chopped fresh basil
1 teaspoon chopped fresh oregano

Heat the oil in a large, heavy skillet over medium-high heat. Add the mushrooms, salt, and pepper, and cook, stirring, until the mushrooms are wilted and begin to caramelize. Add the shallots and garlic, and cook, stirring, for 30 seconds. Add the wine and cook, stirring to loosen any browned bits in the pan, until the liquid has almost evaporated, about 2 minutes. Remove from the heat and transfer the mushrooms to the bowl of a food processor. Add the cheese, bread crumbs, parsley, basil, and oregano, and process on high speed to make a thick paste. Transfer to a bowl and divide into four equal portions. Roll each into a firm ball and use to stuff the chicken breasts.

CHICKEN

4 boneless, skinless chicken breast halves
Wild Mushroom Stuffing (above)
Salt and pepper to taste
2 tablespoons olive oil
½ cup finely chopped shallots
1 teaspoon minced garlic
1 tablespoon chopped fresh thyme leaves
¼ cup Madeira
2 cups chicken stock

Preheat the oven to 400°F.

Place the chicken breast between sheets of plastic wrap or waxed paper and, with the flat side of a meat mallet, pound them to ¼-inch thickness. Pat dry with paper towels. Place one ball of mushroom stuffing along half of each chicken breast. Tuck the short ends in and roll up the chicken into a tight cylinder. Fasten with toothpicks. Season with salt and pepper.

In a large, nonstick skillet, heat the oil over high heat. Add the stuffed chicken and cook, turning frequently, until brown on all sides, 3–4 minutes. Remove from the heat and place in the oven. Bake until cooked through, about 7 minutes. Remove from the oven. (Alternatively, cover the skillet and cook over low heat until the chicken is cooked through, about 6 minutes.) Transfer the chicken to a plate and cover to keep warm.

Add the shallots to the pan juices and cook over medium heat until soft`, about 3 minutes. Add the garlic and thyme and cook, stirring, for 30 seconds. Add the Madeira and bring to a boil. Cook, stirring, until reduced by half, about 2 minutes. Add the chicken stock, return to a boil, and cook until reduced by half, about 6 minutes. Add the chicken and any juices to the pan and cook until the chicken is warmed through, about 1 minute.

CHEF'S NOTES:

Great served with mashed potatoes or Roquefort cheese polenta.

VARIATIONS:

Can be made with pork, veal, or lamb. The stuffing can also be served as a side dish.

BEST SEASON:

This is a great dish for fall and winter.

BACON-WRAPPED PORK TENDERLOIN WITH WILD MUSHROOM RISOTTO AND RED WINE DEMI-GLACE

Taking the time to make a red wine demi-glace indicates that you put a lot of love into your meal. Whether you are creating it for your family or for a dinner party, this bite uses really special ingredients. Enjoy!

EXPERIENCE LEVEL: ③
YIELD: 4–6 SERVINGS

RED WINE DEMI-GLACE

3 pounds assorted veal bones
½ carrot, peeled and roughly chopped
1 small onion, peeled and roughly chopped
1 celery stalk, roughly chopped
1 bouquet garni
Canola spray
¼ cup finely chopped shallots
2 garlic cloves, finely chopped
¼ cup red Burgundy wine
2 tablespoons dry sherry
¼ teaspoon salt
1½ teaspoons freshly ground black pepper
1 tablespoon cornstarch

Preheat the oven to 350°F.

Spread bones, carrot, onion, and celery on a rimmed baking sheet. Roast, tossing several times, until vegetables and bones have begun to take on color, about 1 hour. Transfer roasted vegetables and bones to a 5-quart stockpot. Add 2 quarts water and bouquet garni and bring to a boil. Reduce heat and simmer gently, uncovered, until the liquid measures approximately 2 cups, about 2 hours. Remove and discard bones and bouquet garni. Strain out vegetables and reserve liquid. Use gravy separator to skim fat (or let cool, then refrigerate until fat has solidified, at least 2 hours, and lift off and discard fat).

Spray a large sauté pan with canola oil and set over medium heat. Add shallots and garlic and cook, stirring, until shallots are translucent. Add wine and sherry and simmer, stirring and scraping up browned bits from bottom of pan, until wines are almost evaporated, about 4 minutes. Add defatted cooking liquid and ¾ cup water. Bring to a boil and simmer until reduced to about 2 cups, about 5 minutes. Season with salt and pepper.

In a small bowl, stir together cornstarch and 1 tablespoon water to form a paste. Stir paste into liquid and continue to simmer until thickened, about 1 minute more. At serving time, drizzle demi-glace on and around meat.

BACON-WRAPPED PORK TENDERLOIN

1 head garlic, top sliced off
4 tablespoons olive oil, divided
2 (1–1½-pound) pork tenderloins, trimmed of
    excess fat
Salt and freshly ground black pepper to taste
1 tablespoon chopped fresh rosemary leaves
12 chopped fresh sage leaves,
1 tablespoon chopped fresh thyme leaves
12 (¼-inch-thick) bacon slices

Preheat the oven to 300°F.

Place garlic in a small ramekin, drizzle with 1 tablespoon olive oil, and wrap in foil. Bake until soft, about 45 minutes. When cool enough to handle, squeeze garlic flesh into a small bowl.

Place tenderloins on work surface. Rub their tops with the roasted garlic and season with salt and pepper. Mix together the herbs and scatter over the garlic on the tenderloins. Wrap 6 bacon strips around each tenderloin, and tie the bacon in place with kitchen twine.

Preheat oven to 375°F. Heat remaining oil in a skillet over medium-high heat. Sear the tenderloins until golden brown on all sides. Transfer seared tenderloins to a roasting pan; place in the oven, and cook to medium doneness, 8–10 minutes or until the internal temperature is 150°F. Transfer tenderloins to a cutting board and let stand 10 minutes. Remove twine before carving.

WILD MUSHROOM RISOTTO

9½ tablespoons unsalted butter, divided

1½ pounds fresh wild mushrooms (such as cèpe/porcini, hen of the woods, chanterelle, or stemmed shiitake), large mushrooms sliced, small mushrooms halved or quartered

Salt and pepper to taste

Approximately 7 cups low-sodium chicken broth

1 tablespoon extra-virgin olive oil

¾ cup finely chopped leeks

1¼ cups arborio rice

¼ cup dry white wine

¼ cup dry white vermouth

¼ cup grated Parmesan cheese, plus additional for serving (optional)

Melt 2 tablespoons butter in a heavy, large skillet over medium-high heat. Add one-fourth of the mushrooms and sprinkle with salt and pepper. Sauté mushrooms until tender and beginning to brown, 3–4 minutes. Transfer mushrooms to a medium bowl. Working in three batches, repeat with 6 more tablespoons butter, remaining mushrooms, and salt and pepper.

Bring 7 cups chicken broth to a simmer in a medium saucepan; keep warm. Melt remaining 1½ tablespoons butter with olive oil in a heavy, large saucepan over medium-low heat. Add leeks, sprinkle with salt, and sauté until tender, 4–5 minutes. Add rice and increase heat to medium. Stir until edges of rice begin to look translucent, 3–4 minutes. Add white wine and vermouth and stir until liquid is absorbed, about 1 minute. Add ¾ cup warm chicken broth; stir until almost all broth is absorbed, about 1 minute. Continue adding broth by ¾ cupfuls, stirring until almost all broth is absorbed before adding more, until rice is halfway cooked, about 10 minutes. Stir in sautéed mushrooms. Continue adding ¾ cup broth at a time, stirring until almost all broth is absorbed before adding more, until rice is tender but still firm to the bite, and risotto is creamy, about another 10 minutes. Stir in ¼ cup grated Parmesan cheese, if using.

ASSEMBLY:

Spoon wild mushroom risotto onto plates. Slice pork into ½-inch rounds and set on top of risotto. Spoon demi-glace on and around pork and serve.

CHEF'S NOTES:

While there are a few steps to this dish, nothing is overly complicated or difficult. If you love to cook like I do, then I believe you will find this a wonderful experience.

VARIATIONS:

Use veal or even beef for this dish.

BEST SEASON:

Serve with a Pinot Noir or an IPA as a complement to this great fall and winter dish.

STUFFED ACORN SQUASH

Just because this vegetarian dish is healthy, don't make the mistake of thinking that it lacks a punch of flavor. It's an impressive presentation, and the fact that the acorn squash is its own bowl is only part of the fun!

EXPERIENCE LEVEL: ①
YIELD: 4 SERVINGS

1 medium acorn squash

½ cup brown sugar

½ cup plus 2 teaspoons olive oil, divided

Salt and pepper to taste

½ cup quartered brussels sprouts

½ cup thinly sliced oyster mushrooms

½ cup garlic, cloves left whole

½ cup dried cranberries

½ cup cooked, peeled, and lightly chopped chestnuts

½ cup vegetable stock

Preheat the oven to 350°F.

Cut the top off the acorn squash. Slice the bottom of the squash so it will balance and not tip over. Scoop out the seeds. Combine brown sugar, 2 teaspoons oil, salt, and pepper, and rub mixture inside and outside of squash. Cook squash on a sheet pan 20–30 minutes or until tender.

In the meantime prepare all of the other vegetables.

Heat a sauté pan with the remaining ½ cup olive oil over medium heat. Add brussels sprouts, mushrooms, and garlic and sauté until golden brown and tender, about 8–10 minutes. Add dried cranberries and chestnuts and sauté until cranberries and chestnuts are warm. Add vegetable stock and simmer for 4 minutes.

Place acorn squash in the center of a serving plate. Fill with vegetable mix and sprinkle the remaining vegetables around the sides. Keep warm until ready to serve. After presentation, cut squash into quarters.

CHEF'S NOTES:

All prep can be done up to two days before serving, but the same day is preferable. This dish can accompany a meal as a side or be used as part of a buffet.

VARIATIONS:

Use different types of squash, like butternut squash.

BEST SEASON:

This a great fall and winter dish.

ZUCCHINI "LASAGNA" ROLLS

Using vegetables in the place of pasta makes this dish light and gluten-free. I slice the zucchini lengthwise into thin slices and then grill them just until they are pliable.

EXPERIENCE LEVEL: ②
YIELD: 4–6 SERVINGS

CAULIFLOWER PUREE

3 garlic cloves

2 tablespoons olive oil

1 medium head of cauliflower (about 1½ pounds), chopped into florets

1 teaspoon fresh thyme leaves

1 teaspoon chopped fresh chives

Salt and pepper to taste

Preheat oven to 350°F. Toss garlic in olive oil, then roast in aluminum foil for 18–20 minutes, until soft.

Meanwhile, fill a large saucepan with about an inch of water, and insert a steamer basket. Bring the water to a boil, and add the cauliflower florets to the steamer. Reduce the heat to a simmer and cover, allowing the cauliflower to steam 6–8 minutes, or until fork tender. Transfer the steamed cauliflower to the bowl of a large food processor. Add the roasted garlic, herbs, and seasonings, and process to desired texture.

ROASTED TOMATOES

12 plum tomatoes, halved lengthwise, cores and seeds removed

4 tablespoons olive oil

1½ tablespoons Alessi Balsamic Vinegar (or other quality balsamic vinegar)

2 large garlic cloves, minced

2 teaspoons sugar

1½ teaspoons salt

½ teaspoon freshly ground black pepper

Preheat the oven to 450°F.

Arrange cut tomatoes on a sheet pan, cut sides up, in a single layer. Drizzle with olive oil and balsamic vinegar. Sprinkle the garlic, sugar, salt, and pepper over the tomatoes. Roast 25–30 minutes, until the tomatoes begin to caramelize. Remove and cool for later use.

PESTO

3 large garlic cloves, peeled

½ cup pine nuts

2 ounces Parmigiano-Reggiano, coarsely grated

1 teaspoon salt

½ teaspoon freshly ground black pepper

3 cups loosely packed fresh basil leaves

⅔ cup extra-virgin olive oil

With food processor running, drop in garlic and finely chop. Stop motor and add nuts, cheese, salt, pepper, and basil, then process until finely chopped. With motor running, add oil, blending until incorporated.

BROCCOLINI

1 bunch broccolini

Heat a large pot of salted water to a boil. Fill a large bowl with ice water. Separate broccolini into spears. Carefully add broccolini to the boiling water and cook 1–1½ minutes, only until slightly cooked through and tender. To test, remove a piece with a slotted spoon, dip it into the ice bath to cool quickly, then eat it. If the test is good, scoop out the broccolini and immediately move to the ice bath. Keep the vegetables in the ice bath just until they've cooled, 20–30 seconds. Remove, drain in a colander, and set aside until ready to serve.

ZUCCHINI

4 medium zucchini, washed and cut lengthwise
  into ¼-inch slices
¼ cup olive oil
1 tablespoon salt
1 tablespoon freshly ground black pepper

Prepare a grill. If using a charcoal grill, fill one chimney and light it. When all the charcoal is burning and covered with gray ash, pour out and spread the coals evenly over the entire surface of the coal grate. Set cooking grate in place, cover grill, and allow to preheat for 5 minutes. If using a gas grill, set to medium heat. Clean and oil the grilling grate.

Brush zucchini all over with olive oil and season generously with salt and pepper. Place on the grill and cook until browned, 5–7 minutes. Flip zucchini. Cover grill and continue cooking until zucchini is softened, 4–5 minutes more, or until tender enough to roll. Set aside.

ASSEMBLY:

Preheat the oven to 350°F.

Lay two zucchini slices on your work surface, "shingling" to cover edge. Spread cauliflower puree on zucchini, and place two pieces of tomato at the edge closest to you. Place a piece of broccolini in between and roll. Place on sheet pan. Heat in oven 20 minutes or until hot. Remove rolls to individual plates, pooling a tablespoon of pesto next to them, and serve.

CHEF'S NOTES:

Everything can be prepared a day or two ahead without affecting quality; this allows you to put the meal together quickly. It will take 20–25 minutes to heat.

To make this a vegan dish, remove the cheese from the pesto.

VARIATIONS:

You can also use yellow squash or eggplant for this dish. When in season (late May until late August) substitute asparagus for the broccolini.

BEST SEASON:

This dish works for every day and every occasion all year.

COUSCOUS-STUFFED TOMATO WITH MINT PESTO

What's better in the heat of summer than a super-ripe, juicy tomato? Maybe one that's filled with toasted Israeli couscous and a fresh mint pesto.

EXPERIENCE LEVEL: ②
YIELD: 6 SERVINGS

MINT PESTO

¾ cup packed fresh mint leaves

¼ cup fresh flat-leaf Italian parsley leaves

2 scallions, thickly sliced

2 medium garlic cloves

½ teaspoon finely grated lemon zest

2 tablespoons extra-virgin olive oil

Salt and pepper to taste

In a food processor, combine the mint leaves with the parsley, scallions, garlic, and lemon zest, and pulse until chopped. With the machine on, add the olive oil in a thin stream and process until smooth. Season the pesto with salt and pepper.

COUSCOUS TOMATOES

12 medium-size tomatoes, washed

¼ teaspoon salt, plus more to taste

1 (16-ounce) box Israeli couscous

1 (15-ounce) can garbanzo beans, drained and chopped

¼ cup toasted pine nuts

¼ cup chopped fresh basil leaves

¼ cup chopped cooked spinach

Zest and juice of 1 lemon

¼ teaspoon pepper

1 shallot, chopped

1 tablespoon olive oil, plus more if needed

3 cloves garlic, minced

¼ cup Italian dried bread crumbs

¼ cup finely grated Parmesan

Preheat the oven to 375°F.

Slice a very thin section off the bottom of the washed tomatoes to allow them to stand. Slice off the tops and scoop out the insides, sprinkling the interior generously with salt. Place them upside down on a paper towel to drain for 30 minutes.

While the tomatoes are draining, pour the couscous grains into a large mixing bowl. Refer to package instructions for the recommended amount of water to cook grains and bring water to a boil. Pour water over the couscous, stir, then cover with a lid so the grains will steam and absorb the hot water. After 5 minutes, mix the garbanzo beans, pine nuts, basil, spinach, lemon zest, lemon juice, pepper, and ¼ teaspoon salt into the couscous.

In a small sauté pan, cook the shallot over medium-low heat with 1 tablespoon of olive oil. As the shallot starts to become translucent, add the garlic and a pinch of salt. If the pan is dry, add more oil. Sauté for 30–60 seconds longer, until you can smell the garlic and it softens. Add the cooked shallot and garlic to the couscous mixture and stir to combine.

In a small bowl, mix the bread crumbs and Parmesan. Spray a 9 x 13-inch glass baking dish with nonstick cooking spray. Spoon the couscous mixture into the tomatoes and top each with bread-crumb-and-cheese mixture, divided evenly. Place the tomatoes in the baking dish. Drizzle a small amount of olive oil over the topping. Bake uncovered 20–25 minutes, or until the tomato skins starts to split and soften. Serve (and eat) right away with mint pesto.

CHEF'S NOTES:

The mint pesto can be turned into a traditional pesto by adding basil and Parmesan cheese.

VARIATIONS:

Remove the cheese to make this dish a vegan option.

BEST SEASON:

This light and refreshing dish is best suited for spring, summer, and fall. When roasted, even not-quite-perfect tomatoes taste great!

SWEET BITES

Anyone who says food can't make you happy hasn't had a really good dessert. Sweets make me happy—to create them, to share them, and of course to indulge in them! Although I'm not a pastry chef, I could have written an entire book on my favorite sweet bites.

Most of my desserts bring back childhood memories of my grandma, holidays, and my first Disney cookbook (I was eight years old). I was inspired and decided to paint my dad's ceiling with chocolate mousse by turning the hand mixer's blades upward. I'm still a big fan of mousse.

I grew up in Brooklyn, New York, with my grandmother Helen next door. She was an incredible cook and made this amazing honey cake that has stuck with me for almost forty years. I am sharing my version of that dessert for the first time in this book (see page 194). I hope you can feel her hugs in every bite! Like all of my recipes, it's simple yet elegant, with plenty of opportunities to twist it into something that is uniquely yours.

SWEET TEA PANNA COTTA WITH GINGER CARAMEL

It's always fun to play with unexpected flavors in a classic presentation. I put an Asian spin on this panna cotta by using green tea and ginger.

EXPERIENCE LEVEL: ②
YIELD: 12 SERVINGS

SWEET TEA PANNA COTTA

2 cups strong green tea, chilled

1 tablespoon unflavored gelatin

¾ cup milk

¾ cup heavy cream

½ cup sugar

2 teaspoons vanilla extract

Stir together the green tea and gelatin and set aside briefly. Combine milk and cream in a saucepan over medium heat and whisk in the sugar. Heat to boiling; remove from heat. Add vanilla and gelatin-tea mixture and stir until gelatin is completely dissolved. Pour into twelve lightly buttered custard cups and refrigerate at least 4 hours until gelatin sets completely.

GINGER CARAMEL

½ cup plus 2 tablespoons heavy cream

2 teaspoons peeled and finely grated fresh ginger

1 cup sugar

1 teaspoon fresh lemon juice

In a small saucepan, simmer ½ cup heavy cream with the ginger for about 10 minutes. Set aside. In another small, heavy saucepan, cook the sugar with the lemon juice over low heat, stirring frequently, until the sugar caramelizes to a light brown color, 10–15 minutes. Being careful to avoid splatters, stir the remaining 2 tablespoons heavy cream into the sugar. Remove from the heat. Strain the reserved ginger cream into a bowl and then whisk into the pot of caramel until smooth. Serve warm or at room temperature with panna cotta.

CHEF'S NOTES:

This dessert is great as a stand-alone or as part of a dessert buffet. You could also make these in an ice cream pop mold, cut them into chunks, and serve with caramel.

VARIATIONS:

Change the tea to another liquid, such as a berry puree or another flavored tea.

BEST SEASON:

This can be made year-round.

FROZEN BLACKBERRY YOGURT POPS

Your kids will enjoy making their own frozen fruit and yogurt pops.
You'll need an ice-pop mold and wooden sticks to make these, but
they are so nutritious and easy to put together, you won't ever buy
commercial pops again. Just think of all the flavors you can create!

EXPERIENCE LEVEL: ①
YIELD: APPROXIMATELY 10
SERVINGS

⅔ cup water

⅔ cup sugar

4 cups fresh blackberries

1½ cup plain nonfat yogurt

5 teaspoons honey

4 teaspoons fresh lemon juice

Bring water and sugar to a boil in small saucepan
over medium-high heat, stirring until sugar
dissolves. Transfer this simple syrup to a small
bowl and chill until cold, about 1 hour.

Place blackberries in a food processor; puree until
smooth. Pour the blackberry puree into a strainer
set over a medium bowl. Using a rubber spatula,
press on the solids to extract as much puree as
possible; discard the seeds in the strainer. Measure
2 cups blackberry puree into another medium
bowl. Add chilled simple syrup, yogurt, honey, and
lemon juice; whisk to blend.

Divide mixture among ten ice-pop molds, each
with a capacity of about ⅓–½ cup. Top with mold
cover, if available, and insert a stick into each.
(If cover is not available, cover the top of the
mold with plastic wrap, pulling it taut; freeze
until partially frozen, then insert a stick through
the plastic wrap and into the center of each
pop.) Freeze pops until firm, at least 8 hours or
overnight. Dip the bottom of the mold into hot
water for 10–15 seconds to loosen pops. Remove
pops from molds and serve.

CHEF'S NOTES:

This is a quick, easy, healthy,
refreshing dessert for all age
groups.

VARIATIONS:

Change the blackberries to
strawberries or raspberries.

BEST SEASON:

Spring and summer, when
berries are at their peak.

STRAWBERRY AND MINT JULEP MOUSSE WITH LEMON BISCOTTI

This sweet berry mousse is complemented by the tart and gingery biscotti. Using the juice and the zest of the lemon gives the cookie a double punch of flavor.

EXPERIENCE LEVEL: ②
YIELD: 4–6 SERVINGS

STRAWBERRY MINT MOUSSE

1¼ cups frozen strawberries
1 tablespoon bourbon
2½ teaspoons gelatin powder
2 egg whites
⅓ cup sugar
1 cup heavy whipping cream
10 fresh mint leaves

In a small pot, heat the strawberries and bourbon. Sprinkle the gelatin over the strawberries and stir until the gelatin is dissolved. Remove from heat and let cool.

Put egg whites in a medium bowl and beat with an electric mixer until frothy. Add the sugar a little at a time while continuing to beat the egg whites until they form stiff peaks. In a larger bowl, beat the whipping cream until stiff peaks form. Place the cooled strawberry mixture in a blender and puree it. Add about 10 mint leaves and blend.

Pour half the strawberry-mint mixture and half the egg whites into the whipped cream and fold together. Pour the rest of the strawberries and egg whites into the mixture and fold together. Spoon into individual serving dishes and chill before serving, about 1 hour.

LEMON BISCOTTI

2½ cups flour
1 cup plus 1 tablespoon sugar, divided
1 teaspoon baking soda
½ teaspoon ground ginger
¼ teaspoon salt
¼ cup chopped crystallized ginger
2 tablespoons grated fresh lemon rind
1 tablespoon fresh lemon juice
3 large eggs
1 tablespoon water
1 egg white

Preheat the oven to 350°F. Combine flour, 1 cup sugar, baking soda, ground ginger, and salt in a large bowl; stir in crystallized ginger. Mix lemon rind, lemon juice, and whole eggs together and stir into the flour mixture. The dough will be crumbly. Turn dough out onto a lightly floured surface and knead seven or eight times. Divide dough in half and shape each half into a log approximately 8 inches long and 1 inch high. Spray a cookie sheet with nonstick spray and place logs 6 inches apart on it.

Combine water and egg white, brush over log tops, and sprinkle with 1 tablespoon sugar. Bake for 20 minutes. Remove to a wire rack and cool for 10 minutes. Slice each log diagonally into ¾-inch slices. Place back on the baking sheet, standing upright. Lower oven to 325°F. Bake 20 minutes, remove to a wire rack, and let cool.

CHEF'S NOTES:

The mousse and the biscotti can be made one or two days before serving. Be sure to store the biscotti in an airtight container.

VARIATIONS:

The mousse can be changed to any berry.

BEST SEASON:

Spring and summer are best for this dessert. It can be made as an addition to a dessert buffet or as a single serving.

COCO CRISP FILLED WITH PEANUT BUTTER MOUSSE

Delicate and moist layers of chocolate cake filled with creamy peanut butter mousse—could anything be better? Well, maybe if you top it with chopped peanuts and shaved chocolate for crunch!

EXPERIENCE LEVEL: ②
YIELD: 10–12 SERVINGS

PEANUT BUTTER MOUSSE

8 ounces cream cheese, softened
½ cup plus 2 tablespoons creamy peanut butter
½ cup sweetened condensed milk
1 cup sifted confectioners' sugar
3¼ cups frozen whipped topping, thawed

Using an electric mixer, combine cream cheese, peanut butter, and sweetened condensed milk in a bowl; beat until smooth, 3–4 minutes. Mix in confectioners' sugar. Using a large spatula, fold in whipped topping. Chill for a minimum of 4 hours before serving.

FLOURLESS CHOCOLATE CAKE

1 pound unsalted butter
1 pound high-quality bittersweet chocolate, chopped
1 cup strong brewed coffee
8 extra-large eggs
1 cup sugar
1 tablespoon vanilla extract
Chopped peanuts and/or chocolate shavings
    for garnish

Preheat the oven to 350°F. Butter the sides and bottom of a 10-inch springform pan and set aside.

In the top of a double boiler, combine the butter, chocolate, and coffee and melt slowly, stirring occasionally, until smooth. Remove from the heat and let cool for 5 minutes.

In a medium mixing bowl, whisk together the eggs, sugar, and vanilla until frothy. Whisk the egg mixture into the melted chocolate until combined. Pour the mixture into the prepared pan. Bake for 1 hour and cool on a wire rack until it reaches room temperature. Remove the sides of the pan, cover the cake with plastic wrap, and refrigerate overnight.

ASSEMBLY:

Once cake is cooled, slice it horizontally into three even layers. Divide the peanut butter mousse in half and spread it evenly on two layers. Stack them together and place the remaining chocolate layer on top. Refrigerate for 2–3 hours to set. Once set, cut into wedges. Before serving, sprinkle with shaved chocolate and chopped peanuts.

CHEF'S NOTES:

This dessert should be put together the day before. Be careful when cutting chocolate cake horizontally, and do not cut it when warm.

VARIATIONS:

Make with vanilla or peanut butter cake for a more intense peanut butter flavor.

BEST SEASON:

This is great for any time of year.

CHOCOLATE CRUMB GANACHE DULCE DE LECHE

Dulce de leche literally means "candy of milk" in Spanish. The quality and freshness of your milk will affect the flavor of your candy, so use the freshest organic whole milk available.

EXPERIENCE LEVEL: ②
YIELD: 8 SERVINGS

CHOCOLATE GANACHE CAKE

¼ pound unsalted butter, at room temperature

1 cup sugar

4 eggs, at room temperature

1 cup chocolate syrup (preferably Hershey's)

1 tablespoon pure vanilla extract

1 cup all-purpose flour

½ cup heavy cream

1 cup semisweet chocolate chips

1 teaspoon instant coffee granules

Preheat the oven to 325°F. Butter and flour an 8 x 8-inch pan, then line the bottom with parchment paper.

In the bowl of an electric stand mixer fitted with the paddle attachment, cream the butter and sugar until light and fluffy. Add the eggs, one at a time. Mix in the chocolate syrup and vanilla. Add the flour and mix just until combined. Pour the batter into the pan and bake 40–45 minutes, or until set in the middle; do not overbake. Let cool thoroughly in the pan.

For the ganache, cook the heavy cream, chocolate chips, and coffee in the top of a double boiler over simmering water until smooth, stirring occasionally.

DULCE DE LECHE

1 quart milk, preferably whole, organic, and as fresh as possible

1 cup granulated sugar

1 vanilla bean or 1 teaspoon pure vanilla extract

½ teaspoon baking soda, dissolved in 1 tablespoon water

1 cup frozen whipped topping, slightly thawed

In a large, heavy saucepan, combine the milk and sugar. Split the vanilla bean along its length and scrape the seeds into the pot, then throw in the pod; alternatively add the vanilla extract. Bring to a simmer, stirring until the sugar is dissolved. When it reaches a simmer, remove from the heat and add the baking soda and water, stirring vigorously. Cool in refrigerator. Place ½ cup cooled dulce de leche in a bowl and slowly incorporate the whipped topping until smooth.

ASSEMBLY:

Remove cake from pan and slice into 2 layers horizontally, then divide in half vertically so you end up with four 4 x 8-inch pieces. Spread dulce de leche on three of the layers, then stack all four layers, leaving the top without the dulce de leche. Once assembled, refrigerate for an hour to set. Remove from fridge and coat with ganache. Put back in fridge for an hour to set before serving.

CHEF'S NOTES:

All of the components of this dessert can be made ahead of time and combined the next day.

VARIATIONS:

This traditional-size cake could be cut down and presented differently, topped with caramel, as shown in photo.

BEST SEASON:

This is a great dessert for any time of the year.

WHITE CHOCOLATE MOUSSE AND BRANDIED BLUEBERRIES

I like to layer this mousse between crispy white-chocolate cookies, repeating the flavor while playing with different textural elements. Note that this dessert needs to be started two days before serving.

EXPERIENCE LEVEL: ③
YIELD: 4–6 SERVINGS

WHITE CHOCOLATE MOUSSE

1½ cups heavy cream
½ cup coarsely chopped white chocolate
½ cup egg whites (from about 4 eggs)
2 tablespoons sugar

Two days before you plan to serve the dessert, heat the cream in a small saucepan over medium heat just until it boils. Immediately remove from the heat. Place the white chocolate in a medium bowl, pour the hot cream over the white chocolate, and whisk until melted and smooth. Cover and refrigerate overnight.

The next day, remove the mixture from the refrigerator and, using a stand mixer fitted with a whisk attachment or a hand mixer, whip it into fluffy, soft peaks. Cover and return to the refrigerator.

In a clean dry bowl, whip the egg whites until soft peaks form, then add the sugar and continue whipping until glossy and stiff, about 30 seconds more. Fold into the white chocolate mixture, and refrigerate until the next day. Then spoon the mixture (or pipe through a pastry bag) into glasses for assembly.

BRANDIED BLUEBERRIES

Juice of 1 orange
¼ cup water
1 tablespoon brandy
2 cups blueberries (frozen is fine)
2 tablespoons superfine sugar
1 tablespoon cornstarch

In a saucepan over medium heat, combine the orange juice, water, and brandy. Bring to a boil, reduce heat, and simmer for 1 minute. Add blueberries and simmer for 2 minutes. Add sugar and cornstarch, stirring continuously using a large egg whisk until sauce thickens. The whisk will turn some of the blueberries to pulp and give the sauce a rich color.

WHITE CHOCOLATE COOKIES

½ cup unsalted butter, softened
½ cup shortening
¾ cup sugar
½ cup packed light brown sugar
1 egg
2 teaspoons vanilla extract
1¾ cups all-purpose flour
1 teaspoon baking soda
½ teaspoon salt
10 ounces white chocolate, coarsely chopped
½ cup coarsely chopped macadamia nuts, lightly toasted

In a large bowl, cream the butter, shortening, and sugars until light and fluffy. Beat in egg; when incorporated, add vanilla. Combine the flour, baking soda, and salt; gradually add to creamed mixture and mix well. Stir in chocolate and nuts. Cover and chill dough for 1 hour.

Preheat the oven to 350°F.

Drop heaping tablespoonfuls of dough onto ungreased baking sheets about 3 inches apart. Bake 12–14 minutes or until lightly browned. Let stand a few minutes before removing cookies to a wire rack to cool completely.

ASSEMBLY:

Lay 3 cookies on a work surface. Spoon 1 tablespoon of mousse between two cookies, then fan as shown or sandwich. Serve berries on the side or add them into each layer along with the mousse. Garnish with white-chocolate shavings.

CHEF'S NOTES:

The cookies can be made a few days ahead, as can the mousse. The blueberries can be macerated a day or so ahead of time.

VARIATIONS:

Raspberries or blackberries are perfect variations to this dessert. Instead of white chocolate cookies, you can also use biscotti.

BEST SEASON:

This dessert is best suited for spring and summer when berries are readily available and at their peak flavor.

CARAMELIZED APPLE, BRANDY CUSTARD, AND CRANBERRY MOUSSE

This would make an elegant dessert for Thanksgiving dinner, either on its own or to accompany your pumpkin pie. The tart cranberries help cut the sweetness of the caramelized apple.

EXPERIENCE LEVEL: ②
YIELD: 6 SERVINGS

BRANDY CUSTARD

1¼ cups sugar, divided

2 tablespoons water

2 eggs

2 tablespoons brandy

½ teaspoon vanilla

¼ teaspoon ground nutmeg

¼ teaspoon ground cinnamon

¼ teaspoon ground allspice

Dash of salt

2 cups lukewarm milk

Heat ¾ cup sugar in a heavy 1-quart saucepan over low heat, stirring constantly, until melted and golden brown. Gradually stir in the water. Divide syrup evenly among six 6-ounce custard cups. Let stand until hard, about 10 minutes.

Preheat oven to 350°F.

Lightly beat eggs in a medium bowl. Thoroughly mix in remaining ingredients except milk, then gradually stir in milk and mix well. Pour the mixture over the syrup in each custard cup. Place cups in a 13 x 9 x 2-inch pan on the middle oven rack. Pour very hot water into pan, around the custard cups, to within ½ inch of cup tops. Bake until a knife inserted in the center comes out clean, about 45 minutes. Remove cups from water. Refrigerate until chilled.

CRANBERRY–WHITE CHOCOLATE MOUSSE

1½ cups fresh cranberries

6 tablespoons granulated sugar

¼ cup water

Zest of 1 medium orange

1 tablespoon orange liqueur, such as Grand Marnier or triple sec

½ cup finely chopped white chocolate

1 cup heavy whipping cream

In a small saucepan, combine the cranberries, sugar, and water. Bring to a boil over medium-high heat. Reduce the heat to medium and continue to cook, stirring often, until the mixture thickens and becomes jam-like, about 8–10 minutes total. Strain the mixture through a fine strainer into a medium bowl, pressing hard on the solids. Add the orange zest and liqueur, and stir. Cool to room temperature.

In a small microwave-safe bowl, melt the chopped white chocolate by heating it in 30-second intervals in the microwave. Stir well with a fork between each interval and cook only until the chocolate is smooth when stirred.

Whip the cream in a medium bowl until soft peaks form. Fold about a third of the whipped cream into the cranberry mixture, then fold in the melted chocolate. Fold in the rest of the whipped cream. Spoon or pipe into six serving glasses or bowls. Refrigerate for at least 2 hours before serving. If you need to refrigerate longer than 2 hours, cover with plastic wrap without touching the surface.

CARAMELIZED APPLES

3 tablespoons unsalted butter

5 spicy-sweet, crisp Macintosh apples, peeled and cored and cut into ½-inch cubes

3 tablespoons granulated sugar, divided

½ teaspoon ground cinnamon

¼ teaspoon lemon zest

⅓ cup apple cider

½ teaspoon cornstarch, as needed

Melt the butter in a large skillet over medium heat. Add the apples to the pan and sprinkle with 1 tablespoon sugar. Sauté the apples, stirring frequently, for 6–8 minutes, just until they start to soften. Sprinkle the apples with the remaining sugar, cinnamon, and lemon zest. Toss the mixture gently and cook over medium heat for an additional 2 minutes, until the sugar begins to caramelize and the apples are crisp-tender. Transfer the apples from the skillet to a serving bowl with a slotted spoon.

Turn the heat to high and add the apple cider to the skillet, scraping up any browned bits. Reduce the heat slightly and simmer the cider and pan juices 1–3 minutes, until the sauce has reduced and thickened slightly. If you desire a thicker sauce, dissolve the cornstarch in 1 teaspoon water, stir it into the sauce, and allow it to thicken for a moment.

ASSEMBLY:

Remove custard from cups and trim into 2-inch square shapes; cut each square in half horizontally. Scoop about ½ teaspoon caramelized apple onto a piece of custard and top with remaining piece of custard. Serve the mousse on the side or use it to top the custard squares.

CHEF'S NOTES:

You can mix the apples with cranberries to create a more intense cranberry flavor. Take it a step further and use dried cranberries as opposed to fresh.

VARIATIONS:

Change the mousse to a chocolate mousse, which will lend itself deliciously to the custard. You can also use pears instead of apples and leave in round shape.

BEST SEASON:

This is a great fall dessert.

GRAPEFRUIT BRÛLÉE WITH GINGER "FLUFF" AND HORNED MELON–SAKE SAUCE

A crispy burnt-sugar crust on tart grapefruit is delightful, particularly when it is paired with ginger. Horned melon lends freshness to the rich flavors of caramelized sugar and homemade marshmallows.

EXPERIENCE LEVEL: ②
YIELD: 4–6 SERVINGS

LEMON-GINGER MARSHMALLOWS

3 (1-ounce) packages unflavored gelatin
1 cup fresh-squeezed lemon juice, divided
1½ cups granulated sugar
1 cup light corn syrup
¼ teaspoon salt
Zest of at least 2 lemons
Finely grated ginger, to taste
1 tablespoon vanilla extract
Confectioners' sugar for dusting

Combine the gelatin and ½ cup lemon juice in the bowl of an electric mixer. Let it sit while you cook the syrup. Combine sugar, corn syrup, salt, lemon zest, ginger zest, and the remaining ½ cup lemon juice in a saucepan and cook over medium heat until a candy thermometer reads 240°F. With the mixer on low, slowly pour the syrup into the gelatin. Once it has all been poured, gradually raise the mixer speed to high. Beat on high until it is very thick and white; this will take about 15 minutes. Turn down the speed, add the vanilla, and bring the speed back up.

Dust an 8 x 12-inch nonmetal baking dish with confectioners' sugar. Pour the marshmallow mixture into the pan, dust with more confectioners' sugar. Cover and let dry overnight.

Powder a cutting board with more confectioners' sugar and cut into marshmallow-size pieces (I use both a rolling pizza cutter and a paring knife). Roll each marshmallow in confectioners' sugar.

HORNED MELON–SAKE SAUCE

Pulp from 1 horned melon (equals ½ cup melon pulp)
½ tablespoon sake
2 teaspoons chopped fresh mint
1 teaspoon grated orange peel
1 teaspoon sugar

Combine all ingredients into a food processor and puree until smooth.

GRAPEFRUIT BRÛLÉE

1 grapefruit
½ cup sugar, granulated

Peel the grapefruit and segment the flesh out. Toss in sugar and caramelize with a butane torch until sugar begins to brown.

ASSEMBLY:

Divide marshmallows onto plates and caramelize using hand butane torch. Spoon 6 pieces of grapefruit brûlée next to marshmallow, then drizzle horned-melon sauce alongside and serve.

CHEF'S NOTES:

This dessert can be put together as shown or served individually.

VARIATIONS:

Use oranges as a substitute for the grapefruit. Use kiwi as a substitute for horned melon.

BEST SEASON:

This is a great light dessert for the summer when grapefruits are in the peak of season.

CHOCOLATE "FLUFF" AND MINT WHOOPEE PIES

Two childhood favorites in one cookie! Whoopee pies meet Thin Mints in this minty chocolate bite.

EXPERIENCE LEVEL: ③
YIELD: 18 PIES

2 ounces unsweetened chocolate, chopped

4 ounces semisweet chocolate, chopped

½ cup unsalted butter

1 cup sugar

3 large eggs

1 teaspoon pure vanilla extract

1 cup all-purpose flour

¼ cup natural cocoa powder

½ teaspoon baking powder

¾ teaspoon fine salt

18 large marshmallows

Fresh mint leaves, for garnish (optional)

Preheat the oven to 375°F. Line a baking sheet with parchment paper or a silicon baking sheet.

Put the unsweetened and semisweet chocolates and butter in a medium microwave-safe bowl; heat at 75 percent power until softened, about 2 minutes. Stir, and continue to microwave until completely melted, about 2 minutes more. (Alternatively, melt the chocolates and butter in the top of a double boiler over barely simmering water; stir occasionally until melted and smooth.)

Whisk the sugar, eggs, and vanilla into the chocolate mixture until smooth. Sift the flour, cocoa, baking powder, and salt into another bowl. Gradually whisk the dry ingredients into the wet ingredients until moistened. Switch to a rubber spatula and finish folding the batter together; taking care not to overmix. Use a small cookie scoop or spoon to drop a heaping tablespoon of batter onto the prepared pan. Repeat to make 36 cookies, spacing them about 1 inch apart. Bake until the cookies spring back when lightly touched, about 6 minutes. Cool the cookies slightly. Transfer half of the cookies to a rack.

Turn the remaining cookies on the pan over, so they lie flat side up. Place a marshmallow on top of each flipped cookie and return the pan to the oven. Cook just until the marshmallow begins to soften and puff, about 3 minutes. Cool marshmallow-topped cookies slightly, about 2 minutes. Top with the remaining cookies, pressing lightly to make sandwiches. Cool whoopee pies completely on wire racks. Serve garnished with fresh mint leaves.

CHEF'S NOTES:

These can be made ahead of time and held for a week in an airtight container.

VARIATIONS:

You can change the flavor profile of the marshmallow to create a different taste, or change the cookie to a brownie.

BEST SEASON:

This great year-round treat is also a fun recipe to make with children.

OATMEAL RAISIN CAKE WITH LEMON-POPPY CREAM

I've always loved oatmeal raisin cookies, so I thought that making the flavors into a fluffy cake would be fun. Decorating the cake layers with a lemon—poppy seed cream turns it into an elegant adult indulgence.

EXPERIENCE LEVEL: ③
YIELD: 42 BITES

OATMEAL RAISIN CAKE

1¼ cups boiling water

1 cup quick-cooking oats

½ cup unsalted butter

¾ cup packed dark brown sugar

¾ cup white sugar

2 eggs

1 teaspoon vanilla extract

1 teaspoon baking soda

½ teaspoon salt

1 teaspoon ground cinnamon

1½ cups all-purpose flour

½ cup raisins

Pour the boiling water over the quick oats and let stand for 20 minutes, until water is completely absorbed. Preheat the oven to 350°F. Lightly grease a 13 x 15-inch baking pan.

Cream the butter with the sugars until light. Beat in the eggs, then add the oats and vanilla, mixing well. Combine the baking soda, salt, cinnamon, and flour in a separate bowl. Add the raisins to the flour mixture and coat them well. Add the raisins and flour to the oatmeal mixture, and stir to combine. Pour the batter into the prepared pan. Bake for 25 minutes, or until a tester inserted near the center comes out clean. Let cool on a wire rack.

LEMON-POPPY CREAM

1½ teaspoons (3 sheets) gelatin

2 tablespoons cold water

¼ cup sugar

3 large egg yolks

¼ cup cornstarch

1¼ cups whole milk

½ vanilla bean, split lengthwise and scraped (throw the seeds in with the milk)

¼ cup fresh-squeezed lemon juice

½ cup poppy seeds

2 tablespoons lemon zest

1 cup heavy whipping cream

In a ramekin, sprinkle the gelatin over the water and let stand while you prepare the cream. In a medium bowl, whisk the sugar and egg yolks together; add the cornstarch, mixing until you get a smooth paste. Set aside.

Meanwhile in a saucepan, scrape the seeds from the vanilla bean into the milk; heat the milk, seeds, and vanilla bean over medium heat until boiling. Remove from heat and add slowly to egg mixture, whisking constantly to prevent curdling (pour through a strainer if this happens). Remove the vanilla bean. Place the egg mixture in a medium saucepan and cook over medium heat until thick, stirring constantly. Add the lemon juice, poppy seeds, and zest, cook another 30 seconds, and remove from the heat. Immediately add the gelatin and stir until completely dissolved.

Place a piece of plastic wrap on the surface of the cream so that it does not develop a skin as it cools to room temperature.

When the pastry cream has cooled completely, whip the heavy cream until stiff peaks form and gently fold it into the pastry cream. Cool in refrigerator and reserve.

ASSEMBLY:

Remove cake from the pan and divide in half horizontally, then spread half the lemon-poppy cream evenly on the bottom piece. Cover with the top piece, and refrigerate for 1 hour. Remove from fridge, cut the cake into 2-inch squares, and top with remaining cream.

CHEF'S NOTES:

The lemon-poppy pastry cream and cake can be made two days ahead, refrigerated, and assembled on the day of serving. It is best served at room temperature.

VARIATIONS:

Soak raisins in dark rum for 2 hours, then drain and add to batter.

BEST SEASON:

Fall or winter.

CRANBERRY WHITE-CHOCOLATE FUDGE

Fluffy white chocolate flecked with ruby red cranberries makes this bite not only delicious but also beautiful. Add it to your holiday dessert buffet or include it in your gift tins.

EXPERIENCE LEVEL: ①
YIELD: 16 BITES

1½ cups granulated sugar

⅔ cup whole milk

¼ cup unsalted butter, plus additional for the pan

1 teaspoon vanilla extract

1½ cups white chocolate chips

½ cup sliced almonds, toasted

½ cup dried cranberries

Line an 8 x 8-inch square pan with foil, and butter the foil.

Mix sugar and milk in a heavy 1-quart saucepan. Add butter and bring to a boil over medium heat, stirring constantly. After bringing to a boil, continue to boil the mixture vigorously, without stirring, for 5 minutes. Remove the mixture from the heat. Add vanilla and white chocolate chips, and whisk until the chips melt and the fudge mixture is smooth. Stir in the almonds and cranberries. Spread the fudge in prepared pan. Refrigerate for 6 hours or until firm.

Turn over the pan, remove the fudge, and peel off the foil. Turn over the fudge and cut it into 2-inch squares. Roll into balls.

CHEF'S NOTES:

This can be prepared up to a week in advance and refrigerated in an airtight container.

VARIATIONS:

Make with milk or dark chocolate.

BEST SEASON:

This is a great winter holiday addition to any dessert offering.

BROWN SUGAR–BACON CUPCAKES

If you know me, you know I love bacon, and using it in dessert is one of my favorite ways to prove that everything is better with bacon!

EXPERIENCE LEVEL: ②
YIELD: 18 CUPCAKES

BROWN SUGAR CUPCAKES

4 bacon slices

4½ tablespoons unsalted butter, at room temperature

½ tablespoon bacon drippings (reserved from cooking the bacon)

5 tablespoons dark brown sugar

4 tablespoons maple syrup

1 egg

1¼ cups self-rising flour

Pinch of salt

1 teaspoon baking soda

½ teaspoon baking powder

¼ cup milk

Cook the bacon in a frying pan over medium-high heat. Reserve the drippings and place them in the refrigerator to solidify. Mince ¼ cup of the bacon. The chef should eat whatever is left to assure that the bacon is tasty.

Preheat the oven to 350°F. Line 18 muffins cups with paper cupcake liners.

Cream the butter and solidified bacon fat drippings until light and creamy. Add the brown sugar and maple syrup and beat well until combined. Add the egg and beat until incorporated.

Sift the flour, salt, baking soda, and baking powder together. Add some of the flour to the butter-bacon mixture and combine; add some of the milk. Continue to alternately add the dry and wet ingredients, ending with the dry. Mix until just combined. Fold in the minced bacon. Taste and add more maple syrup if needed for desired taste. Keep in mind that the maple frosting (recipe follows) is very sweet, and the syrup should only be added in very small increments, as large amounts of maple syrup can break a cake batter.

Scoop the batter into the prepared muffin tins and bake until a toothpick comes out clean, 18–22 minutes, rotating the tin after the first 15 minutes for even baking. Let cool completely.

MAPLE FROSTING

4 tablespoons butter

2 tablespoons maple syrup

1 cup confectioners' sugar

Cream the butter and syrup until combined. Add the confectioners' sugar, a bit at a time, and whip at high speed until light and fluffy.

BROWN SUGAR BACON

4 bacon slices

½ cup dark brown sugar

Preheat the oven to 300°F.

Rub brown sugar onto both sides of the bacon slices. Bake 13–16 minutes, or until the brown sugar is melted and somewhat caramelized. Remove and allow to cool. Cut the bacon into 2-inch pieces.

ASSEMBLY:

Spread 1 teaspoon frosting on each cupcake and garnish with a 2-inch piece of brown sugar bacon.

CHEF'S NOTES:

The cupcakes can be made a day ahead and refrigerated in an airtight container. Remember to remove the cupcakes from the refrigerator to soften 10–15 minutes before assembly. This will make it easier to frost the cupcakes.

VARIATIONS:

Instead of maple, make chocolate or vanilla frosting.

BEST SEASON:

This is a great dessert for the fall and winter.

MINI CARROT CAKES WITH CARAMEL AND CARROT SALAD

Carrots have a natural sweetness that is emphasized when combined with cream cheese and caramel in these cakes. The carrot "salad" of fried shredded carrot tossed with white chocolate shavings adds crunch.

EXPERIENCE LEVEL: ②
YIELD: 6 MINI CAKES

MINI CARROT CAKES

¼ cup all-purpose flour

¼ teaspoon baking powder

Pinch of salt

Pinch of ground ginger

Pinch of ground cinnamon

Pinch of ground nutmeg

1 egg white

2 tablespoons packed light brown sugar

2 tablespoons canola oil

1½ teaspoons milk

¼ teaspoon vanilla

⅓ cup packed shredded carrot (about 1 carrot)

1 tablespoon raisins

1 tablespoon chopped walnuts

Preheat the oven to 250°F. Prepare with nonstick cooking spray a 4 x 6-inch loaf pan or 6-inch round.

In a small bowl, stir together flour, baking powder, salt, ginger, cinnamon, and nutmeg; set aside. In a medium bowl, beat egg white, brown sugar, oil, milk, and vanilla with wire whisk until blended. Stir in flour mixture until combined; stir in carrots, raisins, and walnuts. Spoon the batter into the prepared loaf pan and bake 15–18 minutes or until the cake is set and springs back when touched lightly in the center. Cool in loaf pan for 5 minutes; remove cake from loaf pan to wire rack. Cool completely.

CREAM CHEESE FROSTING

4 ounces cream cheese, softened

2 tablespoons unsalted butter, softened

½ cup confectioners' sugar, sifted

1 tablespoon real maple syrup

In small bowl, beat together cream cheese and butter with electric mixer on low speed until blended. Beat in confectioners' sugar and maple syrup until smooth.

CARAMEL

1 cup packed light brown sugar

½ cup unsalted butter

¼ cup evaporated milk

1 teaspoon pure vanilla extract

Pinch of salt

Combine ingredients in a small saucepan over medium heat. Cook, stirring constantly, until smooth and creamy, about 10 minutes (time will vary depending on stove).

CARROT "SALAD"

2 cups canola oil for frying

1 peeled and grated carrot

½ cup white chocolate shavings

Heat oil in a deep saucepan to 350°F. Quickly fry the carrot shreds just until crisp. Remove them from the oil and let drain on paper towels. Once the carrots have cooled, toss them with white chocolate shavings.

ASSEMBLY:

Slice the cake horizontally into three even layers and evenly spread the cream cheese frosting on all three layers. Reassemble and place the cake in the refrigerator for 1 hour. Cut into 2-inch squares and top with carrot salad. Caramel can be drizzled around the plate and/or on top of cake.

CHEF'S NOTES:	VARIATIONS:	BEST SEASON:
Cake can be made and frosted two days in advance. Make the carrot "salad" closer to serving time.	Instead of carrot salad use a combination of apples and raisins tossed in a little bit of the caramel.	Fall or spring.

CRISPY APPLE AND CINNAMON-HONEY MOUSSE

Making your own apple chips takes time, but it's easy. Set your oven's temperature to 85°F, then walk away and leave them alone for ten hours.

EXPERIENCE LEVEL: ②
YIELD: 12 SERVINGS

CRISPY APPLE CHIPS

2 Granny Smith apples

Core the apples and slice them thin, with peel left on. Set them on a baking tray overnight, or a minimum of 10 hours, in an 85°F oven. Alternatively, slice them thin and place in a dehydrator set on high for 6 hours or until dried and crisp.

CINNAMON-HONEY MOUSSE

3 teaspoons unflavored gelatin

2 tablespoons water

1 cup milk

2 teaspoons honey

¾ teaspoon cinnamon

2 egg yolks

3 tablespoons granulated sugar

½ teaspoon vanilla

⅔ cup heavy whipping cream

In small bowl, sprinkle gelatin over 2 tablespoons water; let stand for 5 minutes to soften.

Meanwhile, in a small heavy saucepan, heat milk, honey, and cinnamon over medium heat until bubbles form around edge. In a bowl, whisk egg yolks with sugar; slowly whisk in the hot milk. Return the mixture to the saucepan and cook, stirring constantly over medium-low heat until mixture is thick enough to coat the back of a spoon, about 10 minutes. Remove from heat. Add softened gelatin and stir until dissolved. Add vanilla. Pour into a large bowl. Place plastic wrap directly on surface; refrigerate, stirring twice, until the mixture has the consistency of egg whites, about 1 hour.

In a bowl, whip the cream; fold one-quarter into the gelatin mixture. Gently fold in remaining whipped cream. Pour into twelve greased 2-ounce fluted molds, ramekins, or custard cups. Refrigerate until firm, about 6 hours.

HONEY-CINNAMON GLAZE

4 tablespoons unsalted butter

½ cup heavy whipping cream

½ cup raw honey

½ teaspoon cinnamon

2 cinnamon sticks

Pinch of salt

¼ teaspoon vanilla bean paste, or the seeds scraped from 1 vanilla bean pod (pod discarded)

Place a small but heavy-bottomed saucepan over medium heat. Bring the butter, whipping cream, honey, ground cinnamon, cinnamon sticks, and salt to a boil. Boil for 5 minutes and then reduce heat, stirring frequently. Allow the sauce to simmer at a low boil for another 10 minutes. Remove from heat. Remove cinnamon sticks and stir in the vanilla. Allow to cool.

WHIPPED CREAM

⅓ cup heavy whipping cream
3 tablespoons confectioners' sugar

Make a traditional whipped cream by whipping
cream and confectioners' sugar until stiff peaks form.

ASSEMBLY:

Remove each custard from its ramekin and place on
a dish. Dollop ½ teaspoon whipped cream on top,
add apple chips, then drizzle with honey-cinnamon
glaze; glaze can also be served on the side or in a
separate bowl.

CHEF'S NOTES:

Custard can be made up to two
days ahead and refrigerated.
Apples and glaze also can be
made two days ahead and kept
in an airtight container.

VARIATIONS:

Make with pears in place of
apples.

BEST SEASON:

This is a great fall or winter
dessert.

LEMON CUSTARD WITH STRAWBERRY PRESERVES AND COCONUT CRISP

Finishing this dessert with flaky *fleur de sel* not only balances the sugar in this sweet-tart custard, but it adds a crunchy texture to the topping. A touch of salt brings forth the fruit in the custard and preserves.

EXPERIENCE LEVEL: ②
YIELD: 6–8 SERVINGS

LEMON CURD

5 egg yolks

1 cup sugar

Juice and zest of 4 lemons

½ cup unsalted butter, cut into pats and chilled

Add enough water to a medium saucepan to come about 1 inch up the side. Bring to a simmer over medium-high heat.

Meanwhile, combine egg yolks and sugar in a medium-size metal bowl and whisk until smooth, about 1 minute. Measure citrus juice; if needed, add enough cold water to reach ⅓ cup. Add juice and zest to the egg mixture and whisk smooth. When water reaches a simmer, reduce the heat to low and place the metal bowl on top of the saucepan. Whisk until thickened, approximately 8 minutes, or until the mixture is light yellow and coats the back of a spoon. Remove promptly from heat and stir in the butter, one piece at a time, allowing each addition to melt before adding the next. Remove to a clean container and cover by laying a sheet of plastic wrap directly on the surface of the curd.

STRAWBERRY PRESERVES

Juice of 2 lemons, strained

4½ cups sugar

2 pints ripe fresh strawberries

In a large, deep skillet, pour the lemon juice on the sugar. Gently stir the sugar until completely melted. Cook undisturbed over moderate heat, about 10 minutes. Using a moistened pastry brush, wash down any sugar crystals from the side of the skillet. Add the strawberries and bring to a boil over moderately high heat, mashing them gently, until the preserves reach 220°F (or 8°F above boiling point, depending on altitude), about 10 minutes. Continue to boil until the preserves are thick, 4 minutes longer. Spoon the preserves into three hot 1-pint canning jars, leaving ¼ inch of headspace at the top, and close with the lids and rings. To process, boil the jars for 15 minutes. Let cool to room temperature.

CHEF'S NOTES:

Preserves can be made one week ahead. Crisps can be made three days in advance if kept in an airtight container.

VARIATIONS:

Use other berries, such as blackberries, raspberries, or blueberries.

BEST SEASON:

This dessert is great for any time of the year. It can even be used as an afternoon snack when entertaining.

COCONUT CRISP

3 tablespoons unsalted butter

2½ cups unsweetened shredded coconut
   (reserve ½ cup for garnish)

2 large eggs

⅔ cup sugar

1½ teaspoons *fleur de sel* for sprinkling

2 strawberries, sliced, for garnish (optional)

Preheat the oven to 350°F and line two baking sheets with parchment paper.

Melt the butter in a medium saucepan. Remove from heat and add 2 cups coconut. Mix well so the coconut is well coated with the butter.

Beat the eggs with a mixer on medium speed just until blended. Add the sugar and beat on medium-high until the mixture is light colored and fluffy. Combine the butter-covered coconut gently with the egg mixture and mix well. Drop the batter onto the parchment-covered baking sheets and press down gently on each mound until it is relatively flat;

a teaspoon of batter works well, but you can make them smaller or larger, adjusting the baking time accordingly. Keep about 1 inch of space between each cookie, more if you aren't flattening them.

Bake 7–10 minutes until golden. Remove from the oven and immediately sprinkle the top of each cookie with a pinch of *fleur de sel*. If the cookies sit and cool too much, the *fleur de sel* won't stick; you could apply the salt before baking, but since it dissolves so quickly, you will lose the visual effect of the beautiful crystals and the pleasant crunch when you bite into one. Slide the entire sheet of parchment with the cookies intact onto a wire cooling rack. As soon as they are cool, put them in an airtight container to maintain their crispness.

ASSEMBLY:

Layer two of the crisps with 1 teaspoon lemon curd, top with 1 teaspoon of strawberry preserves, and stack. Garnish with reserved coconut and a slice of a fresh strawberry, if desired.

S'MORES MOUSSE STACK WITH GRAHAM CRACKER

In this recipe everyone's favorite camp snack is twisted to make a plated dessert. The marshmallows are toasted in the oven and layered with milk-chocolate mousse and graham crackers.

EXPERIENCE LEVEL: ②
YIELD: 4 SERVINGS

FILLING

1 (16-ounce) container frozen whipped topping, thawed and divided
6 milk chocolate candy bars, divided
1 cup sour cream
1 cup marshmallow cream
12 whole graham crackers

Combine 1 cup whipped topping and 6 candy bars in a small microwave-safe bowl. Microwave uncovered 30–60 seconds until melted and smooth, stirring after 30 seconds.

Combine sour cream, marshmallow cream, and remaining whipped topping and fold together until well blended. Refrigerate at least 30 minutes or until ready to serve.

MARSHMALLOWS

36 large marshmallows

To toast the marshmallows, preheat the oven to 400°F. Place a 15-inch length of parchment paper on a large round baking stone or baking sheet. Arrange marshmallows on parchment paper, 1 inch apart (do not allow marshmallows to touch each other). Bake 6–8 minutes or until golden brown. Lift parchment paper from baking stone to a wire rack and let cool completely.

ASSEMBLY:

Layer 3 whole graham crackers side by side and spread about 1 tablespoon of each filling (chocolate and marshmallow) down the center of each graham cracker. Top each with 3 pieces of roasted marshmallow, then stack.

CHEF'S NOTES:
Filling can be piped onto the top layer in a decorative manner.

VARIATIONS:
Filling can be made with chocolate mousse or peanut butter instead of marshmallow cream.

BEST SEASON:
Delicious all year.

VANILLA SHORTCAKE AND POACHED RASPBERRIES WITH WHITE CHOCOLATE–RASPBERRY MOUSSE

When I was young, we really couldn't afford fancy desserts. So my grandma created an inexpensive version of strawberry shortcake with leftover cake, frozen strawberries, and nondairy "whipped cream." This is a much more sophisticated and luscious option to serve when you really want to wow them!

EXPERIENCE LEVEL: ③
YIELD: 12 SERVINGS

VANILLA SHORTCAKE

2 cups cake flour, plus more for dusting
1 cup white whole wheat flour or whole wheat
    pastry flour
¼ cup sugar
1 tablespoon baking powder
4 tablespoons cold unsalted butter, cut into
    small pieces
4 tablespoons reduced-fat cream cheese
¼ cup canola oil
1 large egg, lightly beaten
3 tablespoons nonfat buttermilk

Whisk cake flour, whole wheat flour, sugar, and baking powder in a large bowl. Cut in the butter using two knives or a pastry cutter until the pieces are about the size of peas. Cut in cream cheese until it's also the size of peas. Drizzle oil over the mixture; stir with a fork until just combined (the mixture will be crumbly). Make a well in the center and add egg and buttermilk. Gradually stir the wet ingredients into the dry ingredients with a fork until the mixture is evenly moist. Knead the mixture in the bowl two or three times until it holds together.

Turn the dough out onto a lightly floured surface. Dust with flour and roll into an 8 x 10-inch rectangle about ½ inch thick. Cut the edges square using a butter knife. Cut the dough into twelve equal-size shortcakes. Prepare a baking sheet with nonstick spray, and transfer shortcakes onto baking sheet. Bake the shortcakes until puffed and lightly golden, about 20 minutes. Let cool slightly.

POACHED RASPBERRIES

¾ cup sugar
¾ cup water
1 cup fresh raspberries

Place the sugar and water in a medium-size saucepan over low heat to allow the sugar to dissolve. Raise the heat and bring to a boil. Place the berries in the hot syrup and heat through. Strain the berries immediately, reserving the cooking liquid. Return the cooking liquid to the saucepan and boil to reduce by half. Allow the syrup to cool a little, and then add the berries.

WHITE CHOCOLATE–RASPBERRY MOUSSE

1 (10-ounce) package frozen raspberries, thawed
2 tablespoons white sugar
2 tablespoons orange liqueur
1¾ cups heavy whipping cream
6 ounces white chocolate, chopped

Process berries in a blender or food processor until smooth. Strain mixture into a small bowl and discard the seeds. Add the sugar and liqueur, and stir until sugar dissolves.

In a heavy saucepan over low heat, warm ¼ cup cream and the white chocolate, stirring constantly until the chocolate melts. Let mixture cool to lukewarm. Stir in 1 tablespoon raspberry sauce. Transfer to a large bowl.

In a medium bowl, whip remaining 1½ cups cream to soft peaks, and fold it into the melted chocolate mixture, one-third at a time, until no streaks remain.

ASSEMBLY:

To serve, split shortcakes horizontally. Spoon poached berries and remaining sauce onto the bottoms, top with the mousse mixture and replace the shortcake tops. Repeat with more berries and mousse on top.

CHEF'S NOTES:

Shortcake can be made two days ahead. Poached berries can be made and refrigerated two to three days ahead.

VARIATIONS:

For a twist, change to vanilla mousse and use caramelized bananas instead of the berries.

BEST SEASON:

Try this in spring and summer, when berries are at their peak.

GRANDMA HELEN'S HONEY CAKE TWISTED

My love for cooking started with my grandmother. I created this spin on her honey cake in her honor, and each time I smell it baking, it takes me back to her kitchen in Brooklyn.

EXPERIENCE LEVEL: ②
YIELD: 6–8 SERVINGS

3½ cups all-purpose flour

1 tablespoon baking powder

1 teaspoon baking soda

½ teaspoon salt

4 teaspoons ground cinnamon

½ teaspoon ground cloves

½ teaspoon ground allspice

1 cup vegetable oil

1 cup honey

1½ cups granulated sugar

½ cup dark brown sugar, lightly packed

3 large eggs, at room temperature

1 teaspoon vanilla extract

1 cup coffee or strong tea

½ cup fresh orange juice

¼ cup whiskey

½ cup slivered or sliced almonds (optional)

Preheat the oven to 350°F. Generously grease three loaf pans, or two 9-inch square or round cake pans, or one 9- or 10-inch tube pan, with nonstick cooking spray. (For tube pans, line the bottom with lightly greased parchment paper, cut to fit.)

In a large bowl, whisk together the flour, baking powder, baking soda, salt, cinnamon, cloves, and allspice. Make a well in the center, and add oil, honey, white sugar, brown sugar, eggs, vanilla, coffee or tea, orange juice, and whiskey. Using a strong wire whisk or in an electric mixer on slow speed, mix together to make a thick, well-blended batter, making sure that no ingredients are stuck to the bottom.

Spoon the batter into the prepared pan(s). Sprinkle the top of the cake(s) evenly with almonds, if desired. Place the cake pan(s) on two baking sheets stacked together (this will ensure the cakes bake properly without the bottom baking faster than the cake interior and top). Bake until cake tests done; that is, it springs back when you gently touch the cake center. (For tube cake pans, this will take 60–75 minutes; loaf cakes, about 45–55 minutes; round pans 35–40 minutes.) Let cake stand 15 minutes before removing from pan.

CHEF'S NOTES:

Grandma always drizzled a bit of dark rum on the cake prior to serving.

VARIATIONS:

None—don't mess with Grandma's recipe!

BEST SEASON:

This is a welcome treat any time of year.

TASTY COCKTAILS

As a chef and restaurateur, I have the luxury of working with great mixologists (those who create cocktails) who are a lively, energized, and passionate group. They treat their cocktail recipes with the same reverence and creativity as any executive chef. I worked with the very best in the business to create this chapter, which continues to offer new twists on old favorites.

I myself am far from a mixologist, but I know flavors and balance, so that helps. One of my mentors in recognizing the importance of pairing the proper spirit with your meal was sushi chef Yoshi Amayoki. Although he would never divulge his secrets to making sushi rice, he did share with me the importance of sake to the meal. "The balance of the drink must be taken seriously," he used to say. That was a lesson that I've pursued ever since, learning how to pair food with spirits, savory with sweet, bringing out the best in both.

Keep in mind that a tasty cocktail should never compete with the meal but take its proper place in the balance of tastes. Try offering your guests a Mango-Lime Vodka Martini (page 203) as they arrive, cleansing their palate for the meal ahead. Or end the evening with an Apple Mint Caramel Shaker (page 201) instead of dessert. Be bold in your pursuit of the perfect cocktail, and "Cheers" to a spirited evening!

HIBISCUS AND GIN

Hibiscus-flower syrup adds a sweet tang to this cocktail. It blends with the herbaceous gin beautifully as it turns it a vibrant ruby red color.

YIELD: 1 DRINK

Wild hibiscus flower for garnish
1 teaspoon fresh-squeezed lime juice
4 teaspoons wild hibiscus flower syrup
3 ounces gin

Place the wild hibiscus flower in the bottom of a chilled Champagne flute and stand it upright. Add the lime juice and the hibiscus syrup and fill it up with gin.

HOT CHILI COCOA

This cocktail will warm you after a day on the slopes—or wherever! The combination of chocolate and chili powder is intoxicating. Here the chili powder is used to rim the glass of this almond-scented hot chocolate.

YIELD: 2 DRINKS

1 teaspoon chili powder
1 tablespoon instant hot-chocolate mix
4 ounces hot milk
1 ounce vanilla-flavored vodka
3–4 ounces amaretto liqueur

Spread the chili powder on a plate. Lightly dampen the rim of each glass and dip it into chili powder, shaking off any excess. Prepare hot chocolate following package instructions, using milk instead of water, and mix with vanilla vodka and amaretto. Pour into prepared glasses and enjoy.

LAVENDER HONEY AND LIMONCELLO

I love making my own limoncello. The addition of lavender in this version imparts a slight floral aroma that does not overpower the lemon. This will be good for a party, but be sure to plan ahead, as it takes weeks to prepare.

YIELD: 10–12 DRINKS

6 organic lemons
6 organic limes
3 sprigs lavender
2 liters light rum or vodka
6 cups sugar
3 cups water

With a vegetable peeler, peel the lemons and limes, making sure to avoid the bitter white pith. Discard citrus pulp or save it for another use. Put the lemon and lime peels, lavender, and rum or vodka in a container, seal it, and let it stand for 4 weeks.

Strain the mixture into a container. Mix the sugar and water in a medium saucepan and bring to a boil. Reduce the heat and simmer until the sugar has dissolved. Let cool before adding to the rum mixture.

APPLE MINT CARAMEL SHAKER

Dessert in a glass! You can skip the apple caramel pie and enjoy this decadent cocktail instead.

YIELD: 2 DRINKS

1 cup apple-caramel pie filling, plus 2 tablespoons of juice reserved for rimming the glasses

½ cup apple brandy

¼ cup pitted dates

⅓ cup whole milk

Salt to taste

½ cup finely chopped walnuts, for rimming the glasses

¼ bunch fresh mint leaves, for garnish

Combine in a blender the pie filling, brandy, dates, milk, and salt. Puree until well incorporated. Dip the rim of each glass into the reserved juice and coat with finely chopped walnuts. Fill each glass with the blended mixture, garnish with mint, and serve.

SHAKE AND BAKE

Kids of all ages love milk shakes! Kahlúa and vanilla seem to have been made to complement one another. And of course you need a chocolate-chip brownie to complete the experience.

YIELD: APPROXIMATELY 2 DRINKS

8 ounces whole milk
2 ounces Kahlúa, or other coffee liqueur
3 ounces vanilla ice cream

Place all ingredients in a blender and turn on high until smooth and creamy. Terrific with chocolate-chip brownies.

BAILEYS SHAKE

Baileys in a milk shake? Why not? I think if you can put it in your coffee, you can put it in a milk shake. Serve these at your next St. Patrick's Day party.

YIELD: 2 DRINKS

8 ounces milk
2 ounces Baileys Irish Cream
3 ounces vanilla ice cream

Place all ingredients in a blender and turn on high until smooth and creamy. Wonderful with white-chocolate brownies.

MANGO-LIME VODKA MARTINI

These mango-lime martinis would be the perfect "Welcome" cocktail at your summer pool party or barbecue. And sampling one of these while you are creating your party menu may inspire a tropical twist.

YIELD: 2 DRINKS

MANGO PUREE

2 cups frozen cubed mango
1 teaspoon fresh-squeezed lime juice
⅓ cup water
3 teaspoons sugar

Place prepared mango in a blender or food processor. Add the lime juice, water, and sugar. Blitz well to create a beautiful mango puree.

MARTINI

2 ounces vodka
½ ounce dry vermouth
4 ounces mango puree (recipe above)
¼ cup crushed ice
1 lime, sliced, for garnish

Measure all the martini ingredients into a shaker, including the mango puree. Shake well. Pour out into two martini glasses and garnish each with a slice of lime.

SWEET TEA, VODKA, AND GINGER SMASH

This cocktail is refreshing and zingy. Enjoy any time of year. It would be equally welcome as an addition to your Chinese New Year celebration as it would be on a sweltering hot summer day.

YIELD: 1 DRINK

6 ounces sweet tea

2 ounces green tea vodka

2 ounces ginger ale

Thin slices of ginger for garnish

Combine all liquid ingredients in a cocktail shaker with ice; shake to combine. Pour into a tall glass and garnish with fresh ginger slices.

CRANBERRY LIME TEQUILA TWIST

This tequila lime cocktail with a twist of cranberry would pair really well with a fall-inspired Mexican menu. Experiment by matching it with rich braised turkey mole or a chile-spiced pumpkin soup.

YIELD: 1 DRINK

1½ ounces tequila

¾ ounce triple sec

3 ounces sweet-and-sour mix

Splash of cranberry juice

Juice of ½ lime, plus slices for garnish

Salt for rimming the glass

½ ounce Grand Marnier

Shake tequila, triple sec, sweet-and-sour mix, cranberry juice, and lime juice in a cocktail shaker. Rim another pint glass with salt and transfer contents. Float the Grand Marnier on top, garnish with slice of lime, and serve.

ADULT MILK AND COOKIES

I like to add these milk shots to my coffee stations during events, or present them as a sweet finish at my restaurant. Serving warm cookies will make your guests feel pampered.

YIELD: 4 DRINKS AND 2 DOZEN COOKIES

IRISH MIST MILK

4 cups milk

1 cup Irish Mist

Combine the two ingredients and mix well. Reserve in refrigerator until cookies are ready, then serve.

CHOCOLATE CHIP COOKIES

2 ¼ cups all-purpose flour

½ teaspoon baking soda

1 cup unsalted butter, at room temperature

½ cup granulated sugar

1 cup packed light brown sugar

1 teaspoon salt

2 teaspoons pure vanilla extract

2 large eggs

2 cups (about 12 ounces) semisweet and/or
   milk chocolate chips

Preheat the oven to 350°F.

In a small bowl, whisk together the flour and baking soda; set aside. In the bowl of an electric stand mixer fitted with the paddle attachment, combine the butter with both sugars; beat on medium speed until light and fluffy. Reduce speed to low; add the salt, vanilla, and eggs. Beat until well mixed, about 1 minute. Add flour mixture; mix until just combined. Stir in the chocolate chips. Drop heaping tablespoons of dough about 2 inches apart on baking sheets lined with parchment paper. Bake until cookies are golden around the edges but still soft in the center, 8–10 minutes. Remove from oven and let cool on baking sheet 1–2 minutes. Transfer to a wire rack to cool completely. Store cookies in an airtight container at room temperature until ready to serve.

ACKNOWLEDGMENTS

When Mary Norris from Lyons Press approached me about writing this cookbook, I was excited both to share fun, new ideas and to create a book that speaks to my soul, something that people could use every day for new ideas and inspiration. So thank you, Mary, for this amazing opportunity to create this book and others in the future.

Thank you to my family, for your patience and understanding while I have been working on this book—and all the other projects I have going on! Without you I could never be who I am or have the time to do what I do. 3 always and forever.

To my person, Megan Aldrich, without whom I would never have been able to get a lot of this book done. You helped me every time I had a brain block while shooting, writing recipes, and editing—you rock!

To Jenny, who has inspired me to be better, to push harder, and be without worry. Elephant Shoes.

To my lifelong friend/bandmate/business partner in the Culinary Development and Design Group and the photographer of this cookbook, Tony Calarco. Thank you for all your time and energy. I know it was tough keeping up with me, but look at what we have done.

To Diane McNamara of Fire It Up, PR. Without Diane this book would not be what it is. Thanks for your patience, guidance, and laughter throughout the process. The next one has to be much easier, right? Thank you for your belief in me, in the brand, and in our future. Fire it up!

A special and massive thanks to Christy Hamilton of Fire It Up, PR, for all of your hard work, dedication, and hours spent on conference calls making sure each and every recipe is perfect and home-chef ready. Thank you for all the time you put into other projects such as DC with me, TCC and of course Alessi. Without you I would have never made the impact that we made on them. Your continued and tireless support is appreciated beyond words. And so to you Christy, a big hug and massive THANK YOU!

To my partners Purvi and Akik Shah at Morris Tap and Grill, to my team of amazing people, and to my customers—a big, BIG thank you for allowing me to learn from you, share with you, and be part of your worlds. To my staff at Morris Tap and Grill, thank you all for the support. Your hard work and dedication will always be appreciated and respected. It is my honor to work with you.

To Sarah Plumley at Sarah's Bakery, I know being my partner isn't always easy, that I am never there enough, but I thank you for your patience and friendship with our first year of business. I am proud to call you my partner and friend.

In memory of my catering mentor, Mike Roman—you will always be credited for the turnaround in my career, by teaching me to "stop playing checkers and start playing chess." I miss you, our talks, and your words of wisdom.

This book is dedicated to my grandmother Helen. You are missed every day, you are honored in every way. I only wish you were here to see your great-grandchildren, who would love you and feel the love that I was blessed to have experienced from you. You will always be my safe home. Miss you and your hugs through all the chaos.

Fire it Up!

SOURCES

The condiments you use can make or break your dish. Choose the freshest, cleanest, purest ones you can find. I use Alessi products. They set the benchmark for oils, vinegars, and Italian specialty products, so be sure to check out their entire line at www.alessifoods.com. For the recipes in this book, I've used the following:

Alessi Pinot Grigio Wine Vinegar: *page 10;* Alessi White Balsamic Pear Infused Vinegar: *pages 26, 28, 34, 124, 136;* Alessi Red Wine Vinegar: *pages 82, 140;* Alessi White Wine Vinegar: *pages 84, 140;* Alessi Balsamic Vinegar: *pages 96, 129, 154;* Alessi Ginger Infused White Balsamic Reduction: *page 118;* Alessi Premium Balsamic Reduction: *page 124;* Alessi Orange Blossom Honey Balsamic Vinegar: *page 140*

One of my culinary obsessions is cheese. A few years ago I discovered Joan of Arc cheese, and I've never turned back. They make exceptionally smooth and flavorful bries and other French favorites. You can find most of the line in any grocery store or at www.JoanofArcBrie.com. These are used in the following recipes: Joan of Arc Roquefort: *pages 50, 52, 54, 90, 92, 106, 108;* Joan of Arc Brie: *page 58;* Joan of Arc Goat Cheese with Garlic & Herbs: *pages 70, 100;* Joan of Arc Natural Flavor Goat Cheese: *pages 72, 80, 102;* Joan of Arc Goat Cheese Log with Peppadew: *page 78;* Joan of Arc Goat Cheese with Fig: *pages 90, 92*

Since I work so often in small bites, the picks I use to assemble them are an important part of my repertoire. Here are the specific picks I used in this book so that you can duplicate the look at home. Or check out www.PickOnUs.com to find a wealth of other options that are just right for your style! Bamboo tied heart pick: *pages 7, 45;* rustic bamboo skewer: *pages 15, 49;* reusable wooden fork: *page 19;* knotted bamboo skewer: *page 21;* bamboo tasting cone: *page 29, 35, 65;* double-prong skewer: *pages 39, 41, 43;* mini spatula: *pages 51, 87;* black pick with red bead: *page 61;* red chile pepper pick: *page 63;* reusable wooden spoon: *pages 67, 77, 109;* reusable bamboo fork: *pages 47, 65;* loop bamboo skewer: *page 83;* boat oar pick: *page 91.*

INDEX

ABOUT THE AUTHOR

While most kids were playing with action figures, Eric was in the kitchen testing and tasting recipes. As a youngster growing up in Brooklyn, New York, Eric found excitement, challenges, and passion in his favorite place—the kitchen.

His childhood love became his career path and purpose. He studied at The Culinary Institute of America in Hyde Park, New York, and soon after graduation, worked under celebrity chef David Burke at the River Café. He credits this experience with sparking his creative artistry with food.

Chef Eric believes that food speaks a universal language. To become a truly accomplished chef, one must be aware of the styles of other cultures. Working with chefs from around the world filled his mind with excitement and creativity and opened doors to his future.

The world took notice as Chef Eric became chef de cuisine at the famed Marriott Marquis in New York City. Chef Eric continued to incorporate international flavors while introducing new techniques to his preparation and presentation.

The James Beard Foundation, world famous for reestablishing the American way of cooking and for the practice of using only fresh, indigenous ingredients, recognized Chef Eric for his contributions to the gastronomic culinary scene in the United States. Chef Eric was also invited for the fifth time to host a dinner at the James Beard House in New York for the Great Regional Chefs of America Series, the first catering chef to be given this prestigious opportunity.

The superlatives continued when The International Chef's Association named Chef Eric Creative Caterer of the Year and Chef of the Year—the only American chef to receive that distinction.

Complementing the industry recognition was the tremendous media attention Chef Eric has received. He's been twice featured in *Wine Spectator* magazine with an Award of Excellence. *USA Today* recognized him as one of the Top Ten New Chefs, and the *New York Times* honored his restaurant, Pleiades, with a three-star rating.

Food Art magazine named Chef Eric one of the Top Ten Chefs. He was featured in *Jezebel* magazine in the Top Twenty Chefs of Distinction. *Catering Magazine, Catersource* magazine, and *Chef Magazine* all recognized him for his creative small plate creations and trendsetting approach.

He has made numerous network appearances across NBC, ABC, Fox5, and The Food Network, where he became the 2011 Champion of *Chopped*, the network's highest-rated show. His first cookbook, *Stick It, Spoon It, Put It in a Glass,* is fast becoming a culinary "must" for caterers, restaurateurs, and home chefs alike.

Chef Eric is chef/partner at Morris Tap and Grill, Sarah's Bakery, and partner in Culinary Development and Design Group. A cancer survivor, Chef Eric knows the importance of a support circle in fighting this life-threatening disease. He advocates for the American Cancer Society and has been recognized by the society with its prestigious Heart and Soul Award.

Visit him at ChefEricLeVine.com.